Music in Bulgaria

*M*usic in *B*ulgaria

∞

EXPERIENCING MUSIC, EXPRESSING CULTURE

∞

TIMOTHY RICE

New York   Oxford
Oxford University Press
2004

Oxford University Press

Oxford   New York
Auckland   Bangkok   Buenos Aires   Cape Town   Chennai
Dar es Salaam   Delhi   Hong Kong   Istanbul   Karachi   Kolkata
Kuala Lumpur   Madrid   Melbourne   Mexico City   Mumbai
Nairobi   São Paulo   Shanghai   Taipei   Tokyo   Toronto

Published by Oxford University Press, Inc.
198 Madison Avenue, New York, New York, 10016
http://www.oup-usa.org

Library of Congress Cataloging-in-Publication Data
Rice, Timothy, 1945–
    Music in Bulgaria : experiencing music, expressing culture / by Timothy Rice.
      p. cm.—(Global music series)
    Includes bibliographical references (p.) and index.
    ISBN 978-0-19-514148-1 (pbk. : alk. paper)
    1. Music—Bulgaria—History and criticism. 2. Music—Social aspects—Bulgaria.
I. Title. II. Series.

ML252.R53 2003
780'.9499—dc21

                                                                2003041943

Printing number: 9 8 7 6 5

Printed in the United States of America
on acid-free paper

Contents

Foreword

In the past three decades interest in music around the world has surged, as evidenced in the proliferation of courses at the college level, the burgeoning "world music" market in the recording business, and the extent to which musical performance is evoked as a lure in the international tourist industry. This heightened interest has encouraged an explosion in ethnomusicological research and publication, including the production of reference works and textbooks. The original model for the "world music" course—if this is Tuesday, this must be Japan—has grown old, as has the format of textbooks for it, either a series of articles in single multiauthored volumes that subscribe to the idea of "a survey" and have created a canon of cultures for study, or single-authored studies purporting to cover world musics or ethnomusicology. The time has come for a change.

This Global Music Series offers a new paradigm. Instructors can now design their own courses; choosing from a set of case study volumes, they can decide which and how much music they will teach. The series also does something else; rather than uniformly taking a large region and giving superficial examples from several different countries within it, case studies offer two formats—some focused on a specific culture, some on a discrete geographical area. In either case, each volume offers greater depth than the usual survey. Themes significant in each instance guide the choice of music that is discussed. The contemporary musical situation is the point of departure in all the volumes, with historical information and traditions covered as they elucidate the present. In addition, a set of unifying topics such as gender, globalization, and authenticity occur throughout the series. These are addressed in the framing volume, *Thinking Musically* (Wade), which sets the stage for the case studies by introducing those topics and other ways to think about how people make music meaningful and useful in their lives. *Thinking Musically* also presents the basic elements of music as they are practiced in musical systems around the world so that authors of each case study do not have to spend time explaining them and can delve immediately into the particular music. A second framing volume, *Teaching Music Globally* (Campbell), guides teachers in the use of *Thinking Musically* and the case studies.

The series subtitle, "Experiencing Music, Expressing Culture," also puts in the forefront the people who make music or in some other way experience it and also through it express shared culture. This resonance with global studies in such disciplines as history and anthropology, with their focus on processes and themes that permit cross-study, occasions the title of this Global Music Series.

Bonnie C. Wade
Patricia Shehan Campbell
General Editors

Preface

This book has four main goals. First, it provides an overview of a wonderful music tradition, created and preserved by the accidents of history and the efforts of talented individuals. Modernization and urbanization have dealt serious blows to many rural folk traditions in Europe, but a few, including Bulgaria's, have managed to flourish in the face of the pressure from these trends. Second, it suggests ways for those with and without musical training to engage intellectually and aesthetically with the sound of Bulgarian music. The descriptive language is learnable and understandable by all (see the glossary at the back and the series framing volume, *Thinking Musically*); the musical notations can be ignored or studied, depending on the reader's training and the availability of help from a teacher; and many activities provide suggestions for how to listen carefully and even sing and dance to the music provided on the accompanying CD. Third, the book demonstrates how music, in addition to being an art and an entertainment, is deeply embedded in the cultural, social, economic, and political life of a locale, a nation, and the world. It does this by arguing that, depending on time and place and the history of people's individual experience, music can be an art used for aesthetic satisfaction; a social behavior contributing to gender, kinship, and other forms of relationships; a symbol or text with meaning and reference to a world beyond music; and a commodity with economic value for its composers, performers, producers, and consumers. Fourth, the book offers brief lessons on how ethnomusicologists collect and interpret the musical, social, and cultural material that forms the basis of scholarly inquiry in our field. In this way, readers can learn not only some of the results of research, but how research in this discipline is conducted.

Bulgarian is a relatively easy language to pronounce. The vowels are pronounced like the vowels in Italian: father, met, machine, order, congruent; one vowel has a diacritic above it, ŭ, and it is pronounced like the u in b<u>u</u>t. For example, the name of the wedding band introduced in chapter 1, Kanarite, is pronounced ka-NA-ree-te, not KAN-a-right. The consonants are pronounced basically as in English, except the r, which requires a flipped tongue, as in Spanish, and the h, which is aspirated somewhere between the English h and the German ch. The zh cluster is pronounced like the z in azure, and dzh is pronounced like the j in judge.

This book has benefited from the help of many friends and colleagues over my more than thirty years of research on Bulgarian music. Unfortunately, I can name only a few of them here. I will always be grateful to the prolific Bulgarian musicologist Nikolai Kaufman, who was my "scientific leader-by-the-hand" during my fifteen-month stay in Bulgaria in 1972–73 for my dissertation research. Another Bulgarian musicologist, Vergillij Atanassov, now deceased, has always been helpful, supplying photographs and advice as needed. Many members of the Varimezov family have helped me over the years, but especially important have been Kostadin Varimezov and his wife, Todora, who shared their vast repertoires with me as well as many hours of conversation and friendship. Sadly, Kostadin passed away at the age of 83 on 9 October 2002. Their nephew, Ivan Varimezov, and his wife, Tzvetanka, themselves outstanding musicians, allowed me to use some recordings for this book and helped me make contacts with other musicians and recording companies in Bulgaria. Claire Levy and her husband, Gencho Gaitandzhiev, were especially helpful during my most recent trip to Bulgaria in 2000, and I enjoyed our many hours of conversation. I want to thank a number of Bulgarian recording companies for permission to use their commercial recordings: Balkanton, Bŭlgarska Muzikalna Kompania, Payner Studio, and Magic Film. Also I am pleased that some of the greatest Bulgarian musicians and composers (or their estates) gave me permission to use their music: Phillip Koutev (Elena Kouteva), Stefan Mutafchiev (Nikolai Mutafchiev), Stefan Dragostinov, Kosta Kolev, Atanas Stoev, and Ivo Papazov.

Many in North America helped by giving me permission to use their recordings and photographs: Anna Chairetakis for the Alan Lomax Archive, Yves Moreau, Vassil Bebelekov and his wife, Maria, Karen Guggenheim-Machlis, Georgi Doichev, Flora Grolimund Cannau, and Jill and Jay Michtom. Llyswen Vaughn, Judith Cohen, and Mark Levy helped with contacts and suggestions. Lynn Maners, Carol Silverman, and Vencislav Dimov provided helpful comments on an earlier draft.

A number of graduate students at UCLA contributed in important ways. Angela Rodel was my main research assistant, assisting with musical transcriptions and song texts, checking facts, and reading the manuscript a number of times. Other students who provided helpful comments on earlier drafts of the book were Martin Daughtry, Juniper Hill, and Eva Sobolevski. Pantelis Vassilakis mastered the accompanying CD.

This book is part of a larger project devised by Bonnie Wade. I am grateful for her support during the planning and writing stages. Patricia Campbell, another leader of the project, and several anonymous readers also provided perspicacious and helpful comments. A short-term travel grant from the International Research and Exchanges Board (IREX) supported the research reported in Chapter 7.

To one and all I offer my sincerest thanks. I couldn't have done it without you.

CD Track List

1 The Bulgarian wedding band Kanarite plays *pravo horo*. Balkanton BHA 11111, A1. Used by permission.

2 Maria Stoyanova plays a slow song and *rŭchenitsa* in a meter of 7 (2 + 2 + 3) at a Rom wedding in 1988. Timothy Rice, 1988. Used by permission of Maria Stoyanova, ul. Bosilek 2/10, 4006 Plovdiv, Bulgaria.

3 Bulgarian traditional two-voiced singing from the region around Sofia. Balkanton BHA 11684 B1. Used by permission.

4 Thracian singing with glottal stops. *Bulgaria. Columbia World Library of Folk and Primitive Music* (KL 5378) B1, "Yano Yano," performed by Nadka Karadzhova, age 18, from Thrace. Used by permission of the Alan Lomax Archive.

5 *Zurna* and *tŭpan* from the Pirin Macedonian region of Bulgaria. Yves Moreau, *Beyond the Mystery: Village Music of Bulgaria*, vol. 3, Pirin/Shopluk, track 12c, BMA 1003, BMA Productions, www.bourquemoreau.com. Used by permission.

6 Composition for chorus and orchestra by Phillip Koutev. Balkanton BHA 10420 A7. Used by permission.

7 Popular arrangement of a folk song, "Ela dusho." Nina Nikolina, *Slŭnchogled*, track 3, Bŭlgarska Muzikalna Kompania (no number), 1999. Used by permission.

8 Three-part Shop singing from the village of Vrazhdebna. Timothy Rice, 1972.

9 Band of traditional instruments plays *shopska rŭchenitsa*. Trio Bozhura CD, track 10. Used by permission.

10 Band of folk instruments (*gaida, kaval, gŭdulka, tŭpan*) from the Thracian region playing *daichovo horo* in a meter of 9 (2 + 2 + 2 + 3). Balkanton 10616 A7. Used by permission.

11 Solo *gŭdulka* from Thrace plays a *rŭchenitsa* in 7 (2 + 2 + 3). Balkanton BHA 10616 A3. Used by permission.

12 A slow song (*bavna pesen*) performed by the Thracian singer Radostina Kŭneva accompanied on *kaval* by Georgi Zhelyazkov. Bulgari CD, track 2. Used by permission.

13 Rhodope song, sung by Maria Bebelekova, accompanied on large bagpipe (*kaba gaida*) by Vassil Bebelekov. Courtesy of Vassil Bebelekov, 1999.

14 Two-part drone singing from the Pirin region. Balkanton BHMC 7086 A4. Used by permission.

15 *Tambura* playing a dance melody for *makedonsko horo* in a meter of 7 (3 + 2 + 2). Balkanton BHMC 7086 A1. Used by permission.

16 Christmas (*koleda*) song in meter of 5 (2 + 3). Balkanton BHA 10616 A4. Used by permission.

17 Carnival (*kukerovden*) melodies played on the *gaida* to the accompaniment of bells worn on the costumes of the masked male participants. Balkanton BHA 1045 B1. Used by permission.

18 Easter (*velikden*) dance song in 7 (2 + 2 + 3) from eastern Thrace sung by Todora Varimezova. Timothy Rice, 1978.

19 Harvest song (*zhŭtvarska pesen*) from the Shop region. Balkanton BHA 1293 A8. Used by permission.

20 Sitting song (*sedenkarska pesen*) from the Thracian region. Balkanton BHA 10616 B2. Used by permission.

21 An arranged folk song sung by the choir of the Pazardzhik ensemble. Timothy Rice, 1988. Used by permission.

22 An arrangement of an instrumental suite for orchestra of folk instruments played by the Pazardzhik ensemble. Timothy Rice, 1988. Used by permission.

23 "Polegnala e Todora" (Todora was taking a nap), composed by Phillip Koutev. Balkanton BHA 1103 A6. Used by permission. Rykomusic Ltd. (PRS). All rights for North and South America controlled and administered by Rykomusic, Inc. (ASCAP).

24 An arrangement of *krivo plovdivsko horo* in a meter of 13 (2 + 2 + 2 + 3 + 2 + 2) for solo *kaval*, played by Nikola Ganchev and an orches-

tra of folk instruments. Balkanton BHA 1263, A4. Used by permission.

25 "Zaspala e moma" (A girl had fallen asleep), a song in folk style composed by Stefan Dragostinov and performed by the Phillip Koutev ensemble. Balkanton BHA 11871 A1. Used by permission.

26 A *pravo horo* played by Ivo Papazov and his wedding band, illustrating new developments in the wedding band tradition in the 1980s. *Ibryam Hapazov* [Ivo Papazov], Balkanton BHA 11330 A1. Used by permission.

27 A suite of tunes (incorrectly identified as *rŭchenitsa* in Rice 1994, CD track 42) played by the wedding band Shumentsi at a music festival in the town of Stambolovo. Timothy Rice, 1988.

28 Music by Joe LoDuca for the opening montage of the television series "Xena, Warrior Princess, Vol. 6," Varèse Sarabande Records VSD-6255. Used by permission.

29 Don Ellis's arrangement of *smeseno horo* ("mixed dance") entitled "Bulgarian Bulge." *The New Don Ellis Goes Underground*, Columbia CS 9889 A3. Courtesy of Sony Music and Ellis Music Enterprises, Inc. © Objective Music Co./Ellis Music Enterprises, Inc.

30 *Kopanitsa* in a meter of 11 (2 + 2 + 3 + 2 + 2) played on traditional instruments by a group of American women known as Medna Usta (figuratively, "Sweet Voice"). Courtesy of Karen Guggenheim-Machlis, 195 El Solyo Ave., Ben Lomond, CA 95005.

31 Recording of American women singing the Bulgarian song "Brala moma," composed by Stefan Mutafchiev. UCLA Bulgarian Women's Choir, directed by Tzvetanka Varimezova. Recorded at Pomona College, 2002. Used by permission.

32 Instrumental *kyuchek* in duple meter. Ork. Kristali, *Montana kyuchek*, track 3 (Payner Studio 2005302), 2000. Used by permission.

33 *Popfolk* song, "Every wonder for three days," sung by Boika Dangova. From cassette *Boika Dangova*, A2 (Magic Film AK 087), 1999. Used by permission.

34 *Popfolk* song, "Black Kolyo sat," sung by Extra Nina. From cassette *Byala Kalina*, B1 (Payner Studio 2003286), 2000. Used by permission.

35 *Popfolk* song, "Zet zavryan," sung by Ruslan Mŭinov. From CD *Dŭrpai shaltera*, track 2, Bŭlgarska Muzikalna Kompania (no number), 2000. Used by permission.

36 *Popfolk* song, "Love is a cage," sung by Tsvetelina. From CD *Tsvete da sŭm*, track 4, Payner studio (PNR-9807101-14), 1999. Used by permission.

37 *Popfolk* song, "Do Chikago," performed by Ku-ku Bend. From CD *Nyama ne iskam*, track 4, Bŭlgarska Muzikalna Kompania (no number), 1999. Used by permission.

38 *Popfolk* instrumental, "I nazad," performed by Ku-ku Bend. From CD *Nyama ne iskam*, track 10, Bŭlgarska Muzikalna Kompania (no number), 1999. Used by permission.

Music in Bulgaria

CHAPTER 1

Two Weddings in One Day

∝∾

Bulgaria, a small country about the size of the state of Tennessee, is located in the southeastern corner of Europe on the Balkan Peninsula (figure 1.1). Its population of about eight million people speaks Bulgarian, a Slavic language written in the Cyrillic alphabet. The majority of Bulgarians, ethnic cousins of other Slavic groups such as the Russians, Ukrainians, Poles, Serbs, and Croatians, share the country with minority populations of Roma (Gypsies), Turks, Jews, Armenians, Greeks, and Russians. The music of Bulgaria, with its additive meters, powerful women's voices, homemade musical instruments, and vigorous, intricate dances, has fascinated Americans and Europeans for more than a hundred years. I was first captivated by it in the 1960s, when I learned Bulgarian dances at international folk dance clubs as a university student. I made my first research trip there in 1969 and my most recent one in 2000 to prepare for the writing of this book. In between I have traveled there many times, including for one period of fifteen months.

AN URBAN WEDDING

In 1988, while I was researching another book on Bulgarian traditional music, I had the good fortune to meet Maria Stoyanova (Rice 1994: 268–71). In her thirties at the time, she was a renowned player of the Bulgarian bagpipe, called *gaida* (figure 1.2). On the coming Sunday she was playing at two weddings, and she kindly invited me to accompany her. We were to meet at noon in the lobby of the best hotel in Plovdiv, Bulgaria's second largest city.

At the time, Bulgaria was a rather poor country with a communist government, so I was struck by the hotel's well-appointed interior of shiny mirrors, crystal chandeliers, polished brass accents, and thick carpeting. Surely only tourists and the Communist Party élite could afford to use such a facility. Indeed, the wedding was for the son of a promi-

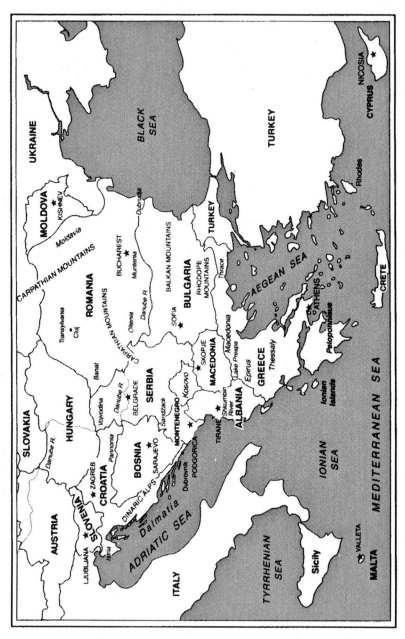

FIGURE 1.1. *Southeastern Europe.* (Copyright 2000 from The Garland Encyclopedia of World Music, vol. 8, Europe, 867. Reproduced by permission of Routledge/Taylor & Francis Books, Inc.)

FIGURE 1.2   *Maria Stoyanova playing* gaida.   *(Cover of Stoyanova 1995)*

nent local government official, and his family was wealthy enough not only to rent the hotel ballroom but also to hire one of the most famous and often-recorded wedding bands in Bulgaria, a group called Kanarite ("The Canaries") (CD track 1).

When Maria and I entered the main banquet hall, the musicians had already set up chairs and a sophisticated sound system on a raised platform beside a medium-size wooden dance floor. Next to the dance floor twenty empty rectangular tables could seat ten people each. The band consisted of clarinet, saxophone, two accordions, electric bass, a typical popular-music drum kit, and a female singer (figure 1.3). Some of the musicians were Bulgarians, and others were Roma, an ethnic minority

FIGURE 1.3 *Kanarite, a famous wedding band, with Maria Stoyanova in the center. Balkanton BHA 11880.*

commonly, but in their view disparagingly, known as Gypsies. Though the name Gypsy suggests that they came to Europe from Egypt, their language and other features of their culture make it clear that they came into Europe originally from India (Liegeois 1986; Silverman 2000).

The band's director asked Maria to play a solo at the beginning of the wedding celebration for two largely symbolic reasons. First, the *gaida* is a powerful emblem of Bulgarian tradition, and weddings in all cultures contain many traditional elements. A common expression claims that "a wedding without a *gaida* is impossible." Although modern instruments gradually replaced the *gaida* at weddings during the second half of the twentieth century, Kanarite hired Maria to evoke a sense of tradition, if only for a short time. Second, it is extremely unusual for a woman to play the *gaida*, and so Maria always caused quite a stir and provoked lots of audience comments when she played in public. Her *gaida* playing helped Kanarite make a memorable impression and contributed to their reputation.

As the guests began to arrive at the ballroom, Maria played a nonmetrical melody, that is, a tune that has no obvious beat (CD track 2).

Such melodies tend to sound rather sad to many American listeners, and indeed such tunes traditionally accompany some of the saddest, most poignant moments in the Bulgarian wedding ritual. One such moment occurs for the bride's family when they present or "give" her to the groom and the groom's family, who then lead her in a procession (or nowadays drive her) to church or a secular wedding hall for the marriage ceremony.

When most of the guests, dressed formally in suits and ties and fancy dresses, had entered and sat down at the tables, the band joined Maria in a tune for the most important traditional Bulgarian dance, *pravo horo* ("straight dance"). All the guests stood up, moved to the dance floor, and formed an open-ended circle, holding hands. The godfather of the couple's future children, called the *kum*, took the hand of the bride, who was dressed in a white gown, and led her to the front of the line (the right end of the line from the dancers' perspective). Led by the godfather, the dance line began to move counterclockwise in an open circle (figure 1.4). The godfather danced especially energetically, with great verve and style, but soon it became clear that he did not know the pattern of steps and was not dancing on the beat, a relatively straightfor-

FIGURE 1.4 *Villagers in traditional costumes dancing a* pravo horo *at a picnic.* (*Timothy Rice, 1972*)

ward duple meter (121212, etc.). As confusion reigned among the guests, his wife, dancing to the left of the bride and smiling indulgently, established a firm model for the rest of the dancers to follow. Soon everyone except the godfather was in sync, repeating together the same relatively simple six-step pattern. At the head of the line, the godfather continued to dance with marvelous enthusiasm but was oblivious to the beat and the dance pattern, expressing his joy at this new union.

Once she had finished the bride's dance, which lasted about a half hour, Maria packed up her *gaida* and we left, leaving Kanarite to play and sing for the rest of the afternoon and probably long into the night as well.

ACTIVITY 1.1 *Learning to dance* pravo horo
Here are instructions for how to dance pravo horo. *Listen to CD track 1, a* pravo horo *played by Kanarite. Find the basic duple meter, the 121212 of the music. Figure 1.5 contains a notation of the first few melodies. First, form a circle and hold the hand of the person on either side of you. The person who leads the dance has his or her right hand free, and so the formation is an "open circle." The leader is at the right end of the line and leads the dance counterclockwise to the right.*

The dance pattern has six evenly spaced steps, which you can count simply as 123456, each step on the 121212 of the music. These six steps then repeat over and over until the music stops. Begin with your weight on your left foot and your body turned slightly (less than 45 degrees) to the right.

Beat 1: Step to the right onto your right foot.

Beat 2: Step on your left foot in front of your right foot.

Beat 3: Step to the right onto your right foot while turning your body to face front.

Beat 4: Lift your left foot slightly in front of your right foot with a slight bend of the left knee.

Beat 5: Step to the left onto your left foot while your body faces front.

Beat 6: Lift your right foot slightly in front of your left foot with a slight bend of the right knee.

Begin the pattern again with step 1 to the right.

FIGURE 1.5 Pravo horo *played by Kanarite, CD track 1.*

A VILLAGE WEDDING

We then grabbed a cab and headed out of town to a nearby village. Villages and their rich rural traditions still provide the foundation for much of Bulgaria's economic, social, cultural, and musical life. Not until the end of World War II and the establishment of a communist government in 1944 did modernization in the form of urbanization, industrialization, and widespread high school education become the norm. The village we went to was situated in the middle of a vast plain extending all the way to Bulgaria's Black Sea coast. The large, well-kept two-story brick houses, with yards and gardens surrounded by fences or stone walls, were signs of the community's relative prosperity. We turned off the paved road through the village and onto a dirt side street. We asked a resident to direct us to the "Gypsy neighborhood." In this village, the Roma, usually the poorest of the poor in Bulgaria, appeared exceptionally well off. As we entered the Rom neighborhood, we could hear wedding music and followed the sound to a huge tent that had been set up on the street between the houses.

Inside the tent, erected especially for the wedding banquet to shield guests from the hot sun, a raised platform held a wedding band similar to Kanarite. A small dirt dance floor separated the band from twenty or so rectangular tables for the wedding guests. Like Kanarite, the band was a mixture of Roma and Bulgarians, including some of Bulgaria's best wedding musicians. As I listened, the clarinet and saxophone players played brilliant solos, amazing their audience and me with their virtuosity. In addition to the guests, a large crowd of Roma had gathered near the stage at the entrance of the tent just to listen; some were recording the music on portable cassette recorders.

We waited while the band played a few dance tunes and songs, and then the musicians invited Maria to play. She began with another non-metrical piece, what Bulgarians call a "slow song" (bavna pesen) (CD track 2). The accordion and guitar players listened attentively and changed chords as the melody progressed. After a couple of minutes, Maria turned to the drummer behind her and signaled that she was about to start the tune for a dance called rŭchenitsa. She then began to play a melody in a meter of seven evenly spaced pulses, combined into three uneven beats counted 1212123 and felt by the dancers as three beats of unequal length: short, short, long (figure 1.6). When the musicians found the beat she established, she nodded her approval.

Constant pulse:	1 2 1 2 1 2 3
Dancers' beat:	1 2 3
Verbal description:	short short long
Musical notation of pulse:	♫ ♫ ♫♩
Musical notation of beat:	♩ ♩ ♩

FIGURE 1.6 *Representations of the* rŭchenitsa *meter of 7.*

Rŭchenitsas are typical of wedding celebrations. Unlike a *horo* or line dance, dancers of the *rŭchenitsa* do not hold hands but move freely about the dance floor, waving their hands or sometimes a handkerchief (figure 1.7). Indeed, the name of the dance is related to the Bulgarian word for hand, *rŭka*. As soon as the musicians had established the *rŭchenitsa* dance beat, a half dozen dancers, both men and women, began to dance individually in the space in front of the stage. Maria's first melodies were song tunes and as a consequence had a rather lyrical quality. The notes in the melodies included a variety of durations from long (half notes) to short (eighth notes) (figure 1.8). The dancers responded to this by dancing in a rather relaxed way with fluid arm and leg motions, with knee flexes that moved their bodies up and down gracefully. After a

FIGURE 1.7 *Two dancers dancing* rŭchenitsa *with a gaida player in the background. (Timothy Rice, 1969)*

FIGURE 1.8 *Maria's melodies for the* rŭchenitsa *on CD track 2.*

minute or so of this kind of playing and dancing, Maria played a long note on the fifth degree of the scale (E), signaling a musical change, and then began to play instrumental tunes that moved with nearly constant, unchanging note values and created a much greater feeling of energy. A few melodies later she increased the intensity of her performance by moving the tonal center of the mode to a higher pitch on the *gaida*. Some of the dancers who heard and understood these musical changes shouted a little yip on "eee" each time and changed their movements as well. They began to make much smaller, tighter movements with less up-and-down motion created by knee flexes. The playing and dancing continued for ten minutes or so, some dancers not matching their movements to changes in the music but others responding enthusiastically to the musical changes, the kind of dancers musicians really enjoy playing for.

As the afternoon progressed, the bride, dressed in a white dress, and her suited groom mingled with the guests. The bride's dress was adorned with a wreath of Bulgarian paper currency (*leva*), pinned on by guests as one way to give gifts to the couple. The guests also gave gifts of money to an MC when they requested a song from the band. The MC then shouted the request and the guests' good wishes on the PA system, often nearly drowning out the music but creating a kind of "joyous noise," called *dzhumbush*, that is an important sonic feature of weddings in Bulgaria. Maria and the band played *rŭchenitsa* after *rŭchenitsa* throughout the afternoon and long into the night.

ACTIVITY 1.2 *Listening to CD track 2*
Listen to CD track 2, a recording of Maria playing a rŭchenitsa *at the Rom wedding described above. Listen for the moments when she holds the long note and then changes note durations and later the melodic mode. Following figure 1.8 may help. Also listen for the general level of "noise" in the recording, including the shouts and yips of the dancers and the announcements of the master of ceremonies. If this were a studio recording, such noise would be absent. But at an actual event, the "noise" is an important part of the fun and an aural sign of the success of the event.*

[margin note: 3 Kinds of Descriptions - objectivity]

EXPLAINING MUSIC

When ethnomusicologists try to explain music, they employ three kinds of descriptions: particular, normative, and interpretive. A *particular description*, as the name implies, focuses on a particular musical event, such as these two weddings in Bulgaria on a Sunday back in 1988. Such particular descriptions sometimes seem as if anyone could write them and as if they are somehow objective, that is, everyone would see and hear more or less the same thing if they attended this event. In fact, such descriptions are always highly selective and depend on what the observer happens to know about Bulgarian music and weddings and thinks is important to convey to the reader. It is a sure bet, for example, that guests at the wedding might be more interested in observing and describing who was dancing next to whom, how good the food was, and how beautiful the bride and her dress were. Thus, particular descriptions always contain elements of selection and interpretation.

Normative descriptions try to capture what is typical about an event and are based on making generalizations after observing many particular events. I could transform the particular into the normative by writing something like this: "At Bulgarian weddings the most important dances are the *pravo horo* in duple meter and the *rŭchenitsa* in a meter of 7." Normative descriptions extract the regularities that recur from event to event and in the process clarify important elements of shared culture that have been performed over long spans of time.

Interpretive descriptions, dubbed "thick descriptions" by the anthropologist Clifford Geertz (1973), combine the particular and the normative and move beyond them to interpret some of the cultural meanings enacted in the particular event. Interpreting meaning—especially the social, cultural, economic, and artistic significance of musical performances—through thick description is one of the most important goals of ethnomusicological research. The following sections examine some normative aspects of these two wedding celebrations and interpret some of the cultural issues being negotiated at these particular wedding events.

THE CULTURE OF MUSIC AT BULGARIAN WEDDINGS

Although several normative ideas lie behind these particular descriptions of Bulgarian wedding music, I focus for now on just two of them. The first concerns the music itself, and the second concerns the social patterning of the musical event.

First, these events included the two basic approaches to meter in Bulgarian music. Nonmetrical songs and instrumental tunes without a strict beat exemplify one approach, and tunes in a fixed meter the other. Nonmetrical melodies are performed primarily when people get together to socialize while sitting around a table. Indeed, the long rectangular tables at both weddings are themselves a normative feature of Bulgarian culture. At social gatherings, Bulgarians do not stand and mingle and move around the room the way Americans do at large parties. Rather, Bulgarians prefer to sit around a long table on which the hosts place food and drink. If the space allowed it, they would ideally sit around one ever lengthening table. Sitting together around a table provides a configuration that nurtures good conversation and good company and symbolically represents and performs the unity of the gathering. Drink helps this performance of unity, as does the playing of slow, nonmetrical melodies or the singing of slow, nonmetrical songs that the community knows. Such songs link this event to events people have experienced in the past.

The other approach to meter in Bulgaria is metrical, that is, many songs and instrumental tunes have a definite beat or pulse that is counted in a particular way (for example, 12121212 or 1212123/1212123). Metrical songs and instrumental tunes are almost always a catalyst for dancing. Furthermore, meter is one of the most interesting features of Bulgarian music, because of the wide variety of so-called "additive meters" such as the *rŭchenitsa* in 7.

A second normative aspect of wedding events is that they always entail the performance of social relationships, especially changing kinship relations. A Bulgarian wedding is not simply the union of a couple in love, as some Americans might conceptualize it, but the union of two families, who ever after refer to one another affectionately as "in-laws." In traditional Bulgarian society, after marriage the bride and groom lived with the groom's parents and family, who assumed an ongoing responsibility for the economic well-being of the new couple. Many aspects of the wedding celebration and its music reflect this old rural tradition even in modern urban contexts. The playing of slow, non-metrical melodies that lament the separation of the bride from her family is one example of this.

THE INTERPRETATION OF MUSIC AT BULGARIAN WEDDINGS

Each particular musical event in a society is not simply the expression and repetition of cultural and musical norms. Rather, people at the event decide precisely what to do, when to do it, and how to do it, and their decisions are subject to scrutiny and interpretation by their relatives, friends, and neighbors. Was the bride's mother dressed appropriately for a woman of her age? Did the groom's brother get too drunk? Why did the band sing that sad song about the unhappy bride? In other words, the difference between particular behaviors and social and cultural norms leads people, including ethnomusicologists, to want to interpret the meaning of those particular behaviors.

Almost every action at the wedding could be interpreted for its meaning. For example, what is the significance of the fact that Roma and Bulgarians play together at both Bulgarian and Roma weddings? Why were the Roma dancing the *rŭchenitsa*, a Bulgarian dance, and not their own solo dance, the *kyuchek*? Some of these questions will be answered in later chapters. At this point, however, I want to interpret just one of the behaviors at these two weddings.

For many Bulgarians, probably the most interesting behavior requiring interpretation at the two weddings was Maria's playing of the *gaida*, since normally (normatively) only men play musical instruments. By examining her individual choice in relation to Bulgarian social norms, the description of the music at the two weddings can be "thickened," and a layer of interpretation missing from the original particular descriptions can be added.

One aspect of culture that musical performance almost always either reaffirms or challenges is the prevailing ideas about gender. Societies differ in interesting ways in their ideas about what is appropriate behavior for each sex. In the United States, for example, this has been an evolving area of discussion and practice for more than a century. Where once symphony orchestras and pop instrumentalists were almost exclusively male, today no one is surprised to see and hear excellent female violinists, wind players, and percussionists in an orchestra or a female guitarist in a rock band. American women, in other words, have achieved a measure of equality in social, political, and economic life generally, and musical performance is one domain of culture where those ideas about equality are expressed and performed visually and aurally.

In traditional Bulgarian rural society, men and women had, and to some extent still have, their distinct spheres of activity, including musical activity. Men, for example, had primary responsibility for taking care of the animals, plowing the fields, building houses, making wine and spirits, and representing the family in the public arena. Women had primary responsibility for cooking food, cleaning the house and yard, making clothing, and caring for children. Music making was linked to these patterns of work. Men and boys spent long hours alone in pastures and forests with their animals; made musical instruments from animal skins and wood; and played them as a way to while away the long hours of solitude. Women's and girls' hands, in contrast, were always busy with housework and thus not free to play instruments. So they learned to sing songs as they learned to embroider, knit, and cook in the social environment of the home among their grandmothers, mothers, aunts, older sisters, and cousins. While men might learn a certain number of songs to sing at the village tavern and when guests gathered together, women, with the rarest of exceptions, never learned to play musical instruments. With all of their domestic responsibilities, when would they have had time to practice?

Maria, however, told me that as a young girl growing up in the 1960s, she was fascinated by the sound of the *gaida*, which her father and uncles played (Rice 2001). When her parents were out of the house, she would take her father's *gaida* from its place under the bed and try to play it. This caused quite a bit of consternation in her family, and they forbade her to play the *gaida*. She kept at it, however, despite their objections and eventually taught herself to play a few tunes on the instrument.

As luck would have it, just as she was about to enter the eighth grade, she received an announcement that the government was inviting students her age to audition for a new high school dedicated to teaching Bulgarian traditional instruments and singing. Thrilled at the prospect, she appeared with her father's *gaida* at the audition, causing an uproar among the jury assembled to judge the auditions.

They were concerned for two reasons. First, if the school was designed to preserve Bulgarian music traditions, then how could they admit a girl to play a musical instrument, since this flew in the face of the very tradition they were trying to preserve? Second, they interpreted her playing of the bagpipe as a kind of sexual act, an interpretation still made by some Bulgarians watching her play. This interpretation, while basically a mischievous misinterpretation designed ultimately to discourage her from continuing to play the instrument, comes from the nature of the instrument. The player essentially "hugs" an inflated goatskin bag and blows air into the bag through a blowpipe. He or she then plays a melody on a melody pipe with seven fingerholes and a thumbhole while producing a drone on a long dronepipe, somewhat suggestively carved, that hangs from the bag (figure 1.2). Amazingly, this jury of sophisticated urban musicians interpreted the blowpipe as a phallus in her mouth. Fortunately for Maria, the jury's interpretations of the meaning of her *gaida* playing did not stop with these two concerns. The communist ideology of the Bulgarian government posited equal opportunity for both sexes. Interpreting Maria's playing as an expression of that ideology, they accepted her into the new high school. Eventually Maria graduated from high school and then entered a newly formed conservatory dedicated to Bulgarian traditional music and song. A few years after graduation, she became the principal teacher of *gaida* at the conservatory. In that capacity, she models and performs the new social ideal of gender equality, introduced after World War II by the communist government. Indeed, the constitution of 1947 called for the "complete emancipation of women" (Crampton 1997: 165).

This new ideal can be problematic, for it puts Maria and other women in conflict with older, traditional ideals about gendered behavior. For example, even though work was traditionally divided in a rather complementary way between men and women, there was a strong sense that men should take a leading role in family and public matters and make the most important decisions. When Maria took a leading role in playing nonmetrical melodies at the two weddings, she forced the male musicians into the musically subservient role of following her to make their chord changes. When she took the leading role in establishing a good tempo for dancing, the male musicians were once again compelled to follow her. Her musically dominant role can be interpreted as one form of social dominance over men in a formerly male domain, a practice shocking to holders of traditional values. A "thick" description of her playing at the two weddings might include the possibility that, in addition to whatever appreciation an audience may have had of her artistic ability, they might have been surprised by the sexual image of her relationship to the *gaida* and the leading musical and social role she took with respect to the male musicians.

What general lessons does Maria's story have for understanding and interpreting musical meaning at particular musical performance events? One lesson is that the interpretation of musical meaning can vary greatly from person to person within a culture. No one meaning can be attributed to music. Maria, for example, simply views her playing of the *gaida* as an art. She plays it because she loves the sound of the instrument. The sexual interpretations are not hers. Rather, they form part of a strategy that some use to try to control her, prevent her from entering this male domain, and maintain the gendered status quo. On the other hand, she does recognize that the *gaida* is, as she puts it, "a leading instrument" and that this is a challenge to traditional views of women's roles in music making and in society. A second lesson is that music is not an art separate from the social, cultural, political, and economic climate that surrounds it and makes it possible. Each particular performance of music also supports or challenges cultural and social norms, such as norms of gendered behavior.

MORE QUESTIONS

Obviously there is much to learn from attending two Bulgarian weddings, even if only for a few hours each. But many questions remain. What other traditional instruments besides the *gaida* do Bulgarians play? Where did the modern instruments in wedding bands come from? Beyond ideas about gender, what were the other effects of communist rule on traditional music in Bulgaria? Why were the Roma dancing Bulgarian dances rather than their own dances? What is going on today? Are Bulgarian youth, particularly those raised in cities and well educated, still as interested in these relatively old forms of music and dance as they seemed to be in 1988? How did I get interested in this music, and what is the nature of American interest in this music? I'll answer these and other questions in the remaining chapters of the book.

Issues:

- acculturation
- Tradition,
  Hegemony
- Gender

CHAPTER 2

The Past in Present-day Music

Events like the two weddings described in chapter 1 are clearly based on traditional practices with varying degrees of historical depth. Some, like the *pravo horo*, are probably hundreds, even a thousand or more, years old. Others, like the elaborate sound systems used by wedding bands, are perhaps thirty years old. Accounting for the history of musical practices is thus an important part of ethnomusicological research. One obvious general principle is that music changes when the social, political, and economic systems that support it change. This chapter looks at the history of Bulgarian music in relation to the country's cultural and political history. As the musical examples illustrate, parts of this past are still present in the music of today.

In 1969, when I first arrived in Sofia, the capital, it immediately struck me that its architecture amounts to a visual history of Bulgaria. Music contributes an aural image of that history. Sedimented in the music, something like fossils in layers of rocks, are musical features from each period of a history that includes the ancient cultures of the Slavs, Greeks, Romans, Byzantines, and Eastern Orthodox Christians; a long period as part of the Ottoman Empire; a central European monarchy; a communist government; and since 1989 an effort to build a multiparty democracy and capitalist economy.

A large Byzantine-style church sits in Sofia's central square, across the street from the headquarters of the Bulgarian Orthodox Church and one of many such churches in the city (figure 2.1). Also in the square is a massive hotel, built during the monarchy from 1878 to 1944 in a central European style, as was the palace of the former king of Bulgaria, now an ethnographic museum (figure 2.2). Near the hotel a huge Soviet-era department store and the headquarters of the ruling Communist Party, built after World War II, express the power of the totalitarian state (figure 2.3). Archeologists have excavated the ruins of the ancient Roman city of Serdica in front of the department store. Farther down the street, a Turkish mosque and public bath (figure 2.4)

FIGURE 2.1 *Alexander Nevsky Cathedral, the largest in Sofia.* *(Timothy Rice, 1969)*

FIGURE 2.2 *The former king's palace, now an ethnographic museum.* *(Timothy Rice, 1969)*

FIGURE 2.3 *Headquarters of the Bulgarian Communist Party.* *(Timothy Rice, 1969)*

FIGURE 2.4 *From right to left, the hotel, department store, and Turkish mosque in downtown Sofia.* *(Timothy Rice, 1969)*

recall the Ottoman Empire, which controlled Bulgaria from 1453 to 1878.

At the beginning of the twenty-first century, these landmarks still stand, referencing the past but significantly changed. After the communist government dissolved in 1989, the red star was removed from the spire atop the former Communist Party headquarters. The Sheraton chain now owns the main downtown hotel. The central department store has been transformed into a shopping mall with private boutiques, and the city has been colorized with the signs of major global food chains and retailers: McDonalds, KFC, Levi Strauss, Gucci, and BMW, to name a few.

If the physical appearance of Sofia contains much of the history of Bulgaria, a few details still need to be filled in, details that begin to account for the particular kinds of music heard in Bulgaria today.

In prehistoric times the territory of Bulgaria was once home to ancient people known as Thracians, Macedonians, and Dacians. Some remains of their languages, art, and material culture have been found, and their names are preserved in modern names for regions of the country, especially Macedonia in the southwest and Thrace in the southeast (figure 2.5). These lands were conquered in the first century A.D. by the Romans. Some evidence suggests that the ancient Greeks and Romans played on bagpipes, and it is likely, though there is no direct historical evidence, that the Bulgarian *gaida* is a survival from pastoral life in ancient Europe.

A flood of Slavic people from northern Europe had inundated these ancient cultures by the sixth century A.D. Traces of ancient Slavic music can still be heard in some Bulgarian music. For example, the loud, tense vocal quality and the two-voice, drone-based textures of some Bulgarian singing resemble some styles of Russian village singing (CD track 3). In parts of Russia and in Bulgaria a characteristic falsetto cry ends each song verse. It doesn't seem too far-fetched to suggest that the similarities in the two styles derive from a shared Slavic culture more than fifteen hundred years old, though as with the presence of the *gaida* in ancient times no historical evidence supports these speculations.

ACTIVITY 2.1 *Listening to CD track 3*
Listen to CD track 3, two-voice polyphonic singing from the region near Sofia. Listen for the melody, the dronelike accompanying part, and the cry ("eee") in the middle and end of phrases.

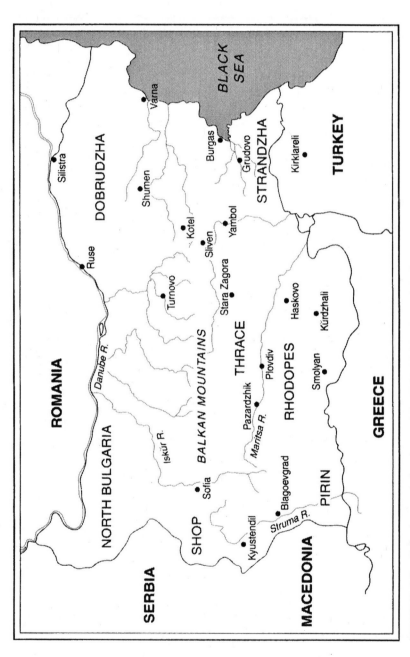

FIGURE 2.5 *Bulgarian musical regions.* (*Rice 1994: 17. Used by permission.*)

Next to arrive in the Balkans were the Bulgars, central Asian horsemen-warriors who invaded in the seventh century A.D. The Bulgars formed the first Bulgarian kingdom in 681 A.D. They must have soon begun to speak the local Slavic language, and they seem to have been absorbed, probably through marriage, into the local Slavic population. As a consequence, they have left little evidence of their culture besides their name. However—and this is highly speculative—they may have brought with them a kind of vocal ornamentation, characterized by quick yodels and glottal stops, that is still heard in Bulgarian singing (CD track 4). This style of singing has analogues in similar techniques from present-day central Asia, Mongolia, and Persia, and may indicate that this style has its roots in Bulgaria's ancient history.

ACTIVITY 2.2 *Listening to CD track 4*
Listen to CD track 4, an example of solo singing from the Thracian region of southeastern Bulgaria. Listen for the glottal stops plus quick yodeling back and forth between the falsetto range and the chest voice.

Bulgarians converted to Orthodox Christianity in 864 A.D., but it is difficult to say precisely how religious chanting in the Orthodox church may have influenced secular singing styles. However, the church's calendar of holidays had an important impact on musical practice in Bulgaria, because the major events in the Christian calendar (Christmas, Lent, and Easter) provide important occasions for secular celebration, music making, and dancing. Also, Bulgarians are often named after Christian saints, and they celebrate their saint's "name day" with a party at home that may include instrumental music, song, and dance.

From the seventh century to the fifteenth century, Bulgarian kingdoms coexisted with and were absorbed by the Byzantine Empire through periods of war and peace until Constantinople fell to the Ottoman Turks in 1453. This spelled the fall of Bulgaria also, and for the next four hundred years Bulgarians were subjects of the Ottoman Empire. This period isolated them from modernizing trends in western Europe and seems to have had the effect of preserving some of the ancient ways of music making described above. It also enriched the country musically, as immigrants and civil servants from the Middle East brought new musical instruments, styles, and practices into southeastern Europe. The Roma, misnamed Gypsies because of the mistaken belief that they came from Egypt, were important carriers of these musical traditions during the Ottoman period. They eventually developed as an important class of professional musicians who performed for the majority population.

The Middle Eastern instruments that came into Bulgaria and the Balkans at this time included a long-necked plucked lute (*tambura*), a rim-blown, end-blown flute (*kaval*), a bass drum (*tŭpan*), and an oboe-type instrument called *zurna* (figure 2.6; CD track 5). Also, the many additive meters, such as the *rŭchenitsa* in 7, so characteristic of Bulgarian music, may have their roots in central Asian Turkic cultures, where

FIGURE 2.6   *Two Rom zurna players.*   *(Yves Moreau, 1979)*

such meters are also common. Finally, many of the oppressive elements of what Bulgarians call the "Turkish slavery" have been recorded in folk song lyrics, affecting the Bulgarian psyche and Bulgarians' view of Turkish culture to this day (Buchanan 1996).

ACTIVITY 2.3 *Listening to CD track 5*
Listen to CD track 5, an example of two zurnas with cylindrical drum (tŭpan), a typical Rom ensemble from the southwestern region of Bulgaria. They play a dance tune called "Deninka" in a meter of 7 = 3 + 2 + 2.

Bulgarians credit the Russians with liberating them from the Ottoman Empire in 1878. From then until 1944, an aristocratic Austrian family supplied the monarchs, called tsars in Bulgarian, who ruled the country. During this period advances were made in industrialization, and an educated intellectual and merchant class developed in the major cities, especially Sofia. Composers and instrument makers came from central Europe to teach Bulgarians European classical music. In Sofia, their students founded a symphony orchestra, an opera company, a music conservatory, symphonic bands, and choruses (Krustev 1978). European harmony and musical instruments such as the clarinet, violin, and accordion began to filter into village music, in some cases replacing traditional village instruments such as the *gaida* and adding chordal accompaniment to traditional solo and unison performance styles.

From 1944 to 1989 Bulgaria's communist leaders undertook massive industrialization projects that caused the majority of the population to move from villages to cities in search of new jobs there. This relatively recent movement of people from villages to towns accounts for why rural, village wedding traditions are still a prominent part of urban musical life, such as the swanky wedding Maria played for in Plovdiv. The government also improved dramatically the educational level of the population in rural as well as urban areas. These developments took a devastating toll on traditional musical life, but at the same time the Communist Party adopted village music as an important symbol of Bulgarian national identity. Government ministries founded professional ensembles devoted to the presentation of "folk music" (*narodna muzika*) in highly stylized and cultivated forms that symbolized the party's progressive goals for its citizens (CD track 6). Through a system of local, regional, and national competitions, they also encouraged villagers to form amateur ensembles to keep rural traditions alive in staged performances (Buchanan 1991, 1995; Levy 1985; Rice 1994: 169–233; Silverman 1982, 1983).

ACTIVITY 2.4 *Listening to CD track 6*
Listen to CD track 6, a recording of a Bulgarian professional ensemble of musicians and singers. A Western-trained composer named Phillip Koutev combined village singers and some of the traditional instruments mentioned above into a chorus and orchestra. Listen for the harmonies, counterpoint, and orchestral textures that characterize this communist-era style of "cultivated folklore."

In 1989 an internal revolt within the ruling Communist Party led to a new multiparty government that has been struggling ever since to enter the world's democratic and economic mainstream. Government support of traditional and arranged forms of folk music has declined, and a new form of popular music that combines Bulgarian traditional music, modern Euro-American pop sensibilities, and Balkan styles from neighboring countries has emerged to address the issues of national and regional identity now facing Bulgarians (CD track 7).

ACTIVITY 2.5 *Listening to CD track 7*
Listen to CD track 7, a recording of Bulgarian popular music recorded in 1999. Notice its combination of synthesized sounds and pop beats with Bulgarian melodies, traditional vocal ornaments, drone texture, and a cry on "eee" similar to those heard on CD track 3.

Thus Bulgarian musical culture at the beginning of the twenty-first century contains elements that link it to the most important periods of Bulgaria's history. Furthermore, it should be obvious that traditional music has never been a static, unchanging, "authentic" form, but rather has changed and evolved throughout its history, depositing sediments of tradition in new practices at every point in time. The ability of music to change and yet retain elements from its past has insured that modern versions of traditional music remain "authentic" to new realities.

CHAPTER 3

A Musical Tour

To create particular, normative, and interpretive descriptions of music, ethnomusicologists typically conduct a year or more of fieldwork. During fieldwork we live with the people whose music we study and attend musical events, both participating in and observing them—a process called participant-observation. We listen to what people say about the music they are making, both in casual conversations and in more formal interviews. We make audio and video recordings and take photographs and detailed notes. To obtain a more intimate knowledge of the details of the musical tradition, we typically learn to play, sing, and dance as well.

Fieldwork can be divided into two basic types: *extensive research*, which surveys a large area of a country or region of the world; and *intensive research* in a single place, often a village or town, for a year or more. A third type, *multisited fieldwork*, combines the two and involves lengthy stays in two or more places. Multisited fieldwork has become more common in the last twenty years as the people ethnomusicologists study move about the globe in search of economic well-being, safety from war and political upheaval, and personal fulfillment.

Over the last thirty years, I have visited most regions of Bulgaria to understand the variety of music making in the country, one goal of extensive fieldwork. The diversity of Bulgarian traditional music is partly the result of geography. The many rivers and mountains that crisscross Bulgaria tended to divide one group of Bulgarians from another, especially in the distant past, when transportation and communication were much more difficult than they are today. On many occasions Bulgarian villagers told me with great pride about the unique features of their local culture. Trying to pull some order out of the variety that exists on the ground, Bulgarian folklorists have identified seven major musical regions, shown on the map in figure 2.5. This chapter contains a metaphorical tour of four of these seven regions—not a complete tour by any means, but enough to give an idea of the range of traditional

Bulgarian instrumental music, song, and dance (see Buchanan 2001 and Rice 2000 for more complete surveys). In each region an anecdote or two illustrates some aspects of the process of attaining knowledge through fieldwork.

THE SHOP REGION NEAR SOFIA

Shortly after arriving in Sofia in 1969, I took a bus to a nearby village on Mount Vitosha in the Shop (rhymes with "hope") region, home to a subgroup of Bulgarians with a distinct linguistic dialect and musical culture. My goal was to meet some village musicians. Using my dictionary and limited Bulgarian, I asked people in the village square if they could introduce me to some *muzikanti* ("musicians"). One woman helpfully pointed me in the direction of the home of a man who played trumpet, and then asked if I would be interested in hearing a women's vocal group that she belonged to. Her response surprised me for two reasons. First, she seemed to understand the word "musician" as referring to someone who played a Western musical instrument and not a traditional one, like the *gaida*. Second, she didn't seem to understand that if I was interested in "musicians" then I would also be interested in "singers."

My first attempt at fieldwork was teaching me what ethnomusicologists know generally, namely, that different cultures have different ways of thinking about and categorizing music and musical behaviors. Whereas Americans tend to regard singers as musicians, through interviews and observation I eventually learned that for many Bulgarian villagers the terms *muzika* ("music") and *muzikant* ("musician") do not include singing and singers. *Muzika* refers to instrumental music, especially professional and Western forms (Buchanan 1996; Rice 1980). The terms *peene* ("singing") and *pesen* ("song") refer to the domain Americans might call "vocal music." This division of what Americans regard as the single category of "music" into two categories corresponds to the social division of labor, mentioned in chapter 1, in which men are almost exclusively the instrumentalists and women are the best singers and the creators of many of the song texts (Blum 2000; Rice 1980; Rice 1994: 115–26).

In 1972–73, when I had learned Bulgarian better, I interviewed villagers for help in understanding the details of their "playing" and "singing." When Shop women get together for communal work in the fields or simply to socialize, they sing very loudly in a two-part polyphonic style (CD track 3). Like Bulgarian researchers before me, I found that the singers had their own words for each of the parts, words that described rather accurately what each singer was doing. For example, they do not use the word "melody" but instead say that the woman who sings the highest part "cries out"(*izvikva*). They do not say that the other singers "accompany" her; rather, they say that they "follow" (*slaga*) or "bellow" (*buchi*), the same word they use for the sound cows make.

FIGURE 3.1 *Three-part Shop song, CD track 8.*

Interviewing singers about their singing eventually led me to a new understanding of the harmonic structure of their singing. Although many Bulgarian scholars and I had concluded on the basis of listening that this was exclusively a two-part singing tradition, the singers taught me that in some villages it is also a three-part tradition (Messner 1980; Rice 1977, 1988). The women who "bellow" do so in two ways: one "bellows crookedly," moving between the tonic pitch and the note below it; the others "bellow straight," that is, sing a drone on the tonic pitch (CD track 8; figure 3.1). Though Bulgarian villagers do not use any kind of musical notation, nor do they have a detailed music theory, they employ enough words to help each other—and ethnomusicologists—understand the structure of their singing, which is difficult to hear.

Whether in two or three parts, the narrow pitch range of Shop songs creates an intensely dissonant effect, at least to most American listeners. However, when interviewed, the singers say the sound is "pleasant" and "smooth." They regard their harmony as, in effect, consonant. The women appreciate the pleasurable aesthetic effect of the clash between the two or three close-together tones. They say they are trying to make the harmony "ring like a bell." To produce this effect, the singers sit or stand close together, and those who "follow" sing into the ears of the one who "cries out" (figure 3.2). This is a good example of

FIGURE 3.2 *Three Shop women singing.* *(Timothy Rice, 1972)*

a truism that ethnomusicologists have long known, namely, that the way people understand and appreciate music, what they find beautiful or ugly, mellifluous or cacophonous, is a product of culture, not something universal.

ACTIVITY 3.1 *Listening to CD track 8 and making intervals "ring like a bell"*
On the recording of three-part Shop singing on CD track 8, listen for the harmonic effect of the close-together tones. How would you describe the harmonic intervals: as smooth, or rough, or ringing, or some other word? (There is no right answer here.) Pair up with a friend who sings in your range and try to sing the interval of a major second. Now try to narrow that interval until you both can hear it ring like a bell. Can you sense when it happens? It is quite satisfying when it does, and you can understand why Shop singers like it so much. Try singing the song from the notation in figure 3.1.

The Shop people are also famous throughout Bulgaria for their fast dancing and instrumental music. They even have their own saying about it: "Beware, Mother Earth, for a Shop is treading on you" (figure 3.3). Fast tempos and, in men's style, high leg lifts and stomps create enormous energy and intensity. The instruments used and the open-circle dance form are similar to those found in other regions of the country (CD track 9).

ACTIVITY 3.2 *Listening to CD track 9*
Listen to CD track 9, a shopska rŭchenitsa in 7 = 2 + 2 + 3. Compare its tempo to the Thracian rŭchenitsa on CD track 2.

THRACE IN THE SOUTHEAST

Across the mountains east of Sofia lies Thrace, a broad plain that stretches from the center of Bulgaria southeast into the European part

FIGURE 3.3   *Shop open-circle dance accompanied by* gaida *and* gŭdulka *(bowed lute).   (Timothy Rice, 1969)*

of Turkey and northeastern Greece. I attended a village wedding there in 1969 and heard a typical Thracian ensemble of *gaida*, *kaval* (end-blown, rim-blown wooden flute), and *gŭdulka* (pear-shaped bowed lute). All three instruments play the melody in octaves, and there is no harmonic accompaniment; even the bagpipe drone is often silenced (figure 3.4). When the dancing began, a Rom drummer appeared and joined the band, playing the *tŭpan* (cylindrical bass drum). He slung the drum from a strap over one shoulder and marked the main beats with a big wooden beater in one hand. He used a thin, flexible wand to fill in the offbeats with a high-pitched sound on the other drumhead (CD track 10).

ACTIVITY 3.3   *Listening to CD track 10*
Listen to CD track 10, a typical Thracian wedding band play-
ing a dance called daichovo horo *in a meter of 9 = 2 + 2 +*
2 + 3. Try to identify the sound of each instrument, and try to

feel the additive meter; the drum may give you the best clue. The first two melodies are transcribed in figure 3.5. Now that you know the names of the main Bulgarian traditional instruments, return to CD track 9 and name each instrument as it takes a solo.

After a wonderful day and long night of dancing, I returned to my hotel in the nearby town, only to be awakened the next morning by a loud knock at the door (Rice 1994: 16–20). A representative of the local Committee for Culture, an organ of the Communist Party, demanded that I meet immediately with the director. I had stopped by to let him know I was in the area before going to the village. He had assured me that all the best musicians were playing at tourist resorts on the Black Sea coast, and so there was nothing much for me to study in his district. This time he was much less friendly and ordered me to leave town, saying, "I thought I told you there was no folklore in [this] district." During the Cold War, each side was deeply suspicious of scholars, travelers, and journalists from the other side. Although musicians, singers,

FIGURE 3.4 *A typical Thracian band of, from left to right,* kaval *(Stoyan Velichkov),* gaida *(Kostadin Varimezov), and* gŭdulka *(Mihail Marinov).* (Timothy Rice, 1987)

FIGURE 3.5   *Thracian* daichovo horo *for band of traditional instruments, CD track 10.*

and Bulgarian scholars welcomed my interest in their culture, the state security apparatus did not, and they watched me carefully whenever I worked there. This specific incident illustrates the more general point that knowledge of others and their musical traditions is never an unproblematic quest for pure information. It always requires the cooperation of those we study and their willingness to share often hard-won and, in some instances, culturally sensitive information with researchers.

The *gŭdulka* played in the Thracian wedding band has a pear-shaped body and a short neck, all carved from one piece of wood. It resembles a big soup spoon. A thin wooden sounding board is glued onto the hollowed-out bowl of the body. The melody is played on three heavy wire strings that run from wooden pegs at the head of the neck over a bridge and down to the tailpiece. Eight or so thinner strings run underneath the three playing strings and are tuned to the main melody notes (figure 3.6). These strings are not played directly but vibrate in sympathy with the played notes, vastly increasing the volume, resonance, and richness of instrument's tone. The *gŭdulka* is held in an upright position on the knee when sitting and supported with a neck strap when standing. The strings are not stopped against the neck of the instrument as players of the guitar and violin do. Rather, the players stop the strings in midair either with the tip of their fingers or, on the highest-pitched string, with their fingernails pressed against the string from the side.

ACTIVITY 3.4   *Listening to CD track 11*
Listen to CD track 11, a gŭdulka playing a rŭchenitsa. Try to clap the basic 2 + 2 + 3 rhythm, which may be hard to hear without the help of a drum accompaniment. The transcription in figure 3.7 may help; notice the constant pulsation on eighth notes, typical of much Bulgarian instrumental music.

FIGURE 3.6 *A gŭdulka player.* *(Timothy Rice, 1973)*

In Thrace I began to learn to play Bulgarian traditional instruments, particularly the *kaval*. The *kaval*, a favorite instrument of shepherds, belongs to the flute family of instruments, though it differs from both the classical side-blown flute and end-blown, whistle flutes like the recorder (figure 3.8). Placing the flute at about a thirty-degree angle to their puckered lips, players blow across the beveled edge of the top end of the empty tube to produce the sound. The tube, made of three pieces, has seven fingerholes and one thumbhole, arranged to play a chromatic scale. It has a very rich sound and a wide range of almost three octaves (CD track 12). Three additional holes at the bottom of the instrument, called "devil's holes" because only the devil plays them, influence the tuning.

Singing in Thrace, unlike in the Shop region, is monophonic. Both men and women sing, but women seem to know more songs than men because

FIGURE 3.7 Rǔchenitsa *for solo* gǔdulka, *CD track 11.*

they are taught to sing them by their grandmothers, mothers, aunts, and older sisters as they do housework. Singing then becomes an important means for women to pass the time as they do household chores and an important way to relieve the emotional stress of daily life (Rice 1994: 115–26).

Perhaps because solo singing is so important, Thracian singers have developed an especially rich practice of ornamenting their melodies with short grace notes and a light vibrato to warm the tone quality on held notes. Singers display their ornamental technique in nonmetrical "slow songs" (*bavni pesni*), such as on CD track 4. Thracian instrumentalists copy these vocal techniques, saying they want to make their instruments sing. Some Bulgarians consider the singing and playing from Thrace to be the most richly ornamented in the country.

ACTIVITY 3.5 *Listening to CD track 12*
Listen to CD track 12, a woman from Thrace singing a nonmetrical song to the accompaniment of a kaval. Listen for her vibrato on some of the longer notes and the way she uses glottal stops as she descends from higher to lower pitches. Notice how precisely the kaval player is able to imitate or "shadow" her singing, even though the song is nonmetrical and therefore he never knows exactly when she will move from note to note.

FIGURE 3.8 *A* kaval *player with his flock.* *(Timothy Rice, 1972)*

THE RHODOPE MOUNTAINS IN THE SOUTH

To the south of Thrace, the Rhodope Mountains separate Bulgaria from Greece. Here men and women sing together in octaves. The song melodies in this region are based on a pentatonic scale (five notes in the range of an octave). The *gaida* is the most important instrument in the Rhodopes and is often used to accompany singing (Levy 1985). It comes in a form almost twice as large as Maria's Thracian bagpipe, and it sounds almost an octave lower. It is often called *kaba gaida* ("big bag-pipe") to distinguish it from the Thracian bagpipe, and it is regularly used to accompany singing (CD track 13; figure 3.9). The instrument is so important and so many men in the region play it that they have a local saying: "If you meet two men on the road in the Rhodopes, at least three of them will play *gaida*."

ACTIVITY 3.6 *Listening to CD track 13*
Listen to CD track 13, a woman singing a nonmetrical song accompanied by the Rhodope kaba gaida.

Bagpipes were once a pan-European instrument, and it is likely that the southern Slavs had the instrument already when they arrived in the Balkans fifteen hundred years ago. The Bulgarian bagpipe is made of a whole goatskin, minus the hindquarters. The skin is cured and preserved by washing it thoroughly in soap and water and then packing it in dry salt for some days. After the salt is washed off, the skin is soft, pliable, and airtight and stays that way for many years. To make the bag, the skin is turned inside out, so the hair is on the inside, and sewn up at the bottom. Stocks (blocks of wood something like a spool) are tied into the two front-leg holes and neck hole of the skin, and three pipes are inserted into the stocks: the blowpipe for blowing air into the bag is placed in one leg hole; the drone pipe, made of three wooden pieces, is placed in the other; and the melody pipe (*gaidanitsa*) with fingerholes is placed in the neck hole (figures 1.2, 3.9). Single reeds—ancestors of the clarinet reed—are inserted into the top of the melody and drone pipes.

To play it, the bagpiper (*gaidar*) fills up the bag with air by blowing into the blowpipe. Pressure from the air in the bag starts the reeds, and the player can play the melody and drone simultaneously. When *gaidar*s run out of breath, they take a breath, but the sound doesn't stop as it would if they were playing, say, a clarinet. The sound continues as they squeeze air stored in the bag over the reeds; a valve in the blowpipe keeps the air from escaping while they take a breath. The trick is to keep a constant pressure on the reeds no matter whether the player blows into the bag or takes a breath. Another trick is to keep your hand relaxed enough to play the melody even as your arm tenses to squeeze the bag. Bagpipes are enjoyable instruments to play, and people seem to enjoy listening to them as well.

FIGURE 3.9   *A Rhodope* kaba gaida *player (Dafo Trendafilov) with singer.*   *(Timothy Rice, 1969)*

The Rhodopes were clearly the right place for me to begin to learn to play the *gaida*, and an accomplished elderly player of the instrument agreed to help me. When I arrived at his house, he and his grandson were playing simultaneously, the old man providing a model and the boy trying to follow as best he could, noodling away in a vague imitation of the ornamentation but with no concept of the melody. The old man invited me to join in, and soon all three of us were making a terrible racket (Rice 1994: 65–68). Listening through the cacophony, I was able to discern the melody and which fingers the bagpiper used to play them. Soon I was able to play a tentative version of the melody, but without any of the ornaments that define the style. The old man suddenly stopped and shouted to his grandson, "That is what you should be playing!"

This incident taught me a great deal about how instrumental music is transmitted in this culture. In most instances, young boys were sent out into the fields to herd sheep and goats and given an instrument such as a *kaval* or *gaida* to help them while away the time. There they had to learn to play on their own. No one could or would slow the music down to teach them the basics. There were no words, such as "melody" or "rhythm," to convey basic concepts. Older musicians had to wait for youngsters to figure out the basic structures of the music on their own. The grandson had clearly been impressed by the rapid finger movements necessary to perform the ornaments in this style, but he had yet to develop any concept of melody and of how to play one on the instrument. On the other hand, I knew how to organize melodies and rhythms from my training in Western music, but it would be years before I acquired the concepts necessary to produce the ornaments so crucial to this tradition. This first lesson was teaching me that, in traditional village culture, the cognitive and motor skills necessary to play instrumental music were learned but not taught.

THE PIRIN REGION IN THE SOUTHWEST

The Pirin Mountains of southwestern Bulgaria are part of a territory known historically as Macedonia. As in the Shop region, two-part singing is also the rule here, but the singers of the second part usually sing a drone on the tonic pitch rather than alternating between two pitches, and the melody singers often use a wider melodic range (CD track 14). These two features combine to reduce the "dissonant" quality of this singing in comparison to Shop singing.

ACTIVITY 3.7 *Listening to CD track 14 and singing it*
Listen to CD track 14 and follow the transcription in figure 3.10.
Now try singing the song with someone with a similar vocal range.
In each verse the line of text is repeated in a slight variant form;
the pattern is the same for each verse. The word mori, *"an emphatic syllable sometimes spoken and sung after women's names,"*
is used as a refrain in the first statement of each line but dropped

> *in the repeat. For example, in the first verse, "Yo Denitse mori Denitse devoi-" repeats as "Ya Denitse Denitse devoiko."*
>
> | | |
> |---|---|
> | Yo Denitse *mori* Denitse divoiko | The maiden Denitsa |
> | Sednali sa *mori* trideset delee | Thirty bold youths were sitting |
> | Sednali sa *mori* kani vino piyat | Sitting and drinking pitchers of wine |
> | Vino piyat *mori* oblag se oblagat | Drinking wine and making bets. |
> | Koi ke mi se *mori* naem dunaeme | Who will take the bet |
> | Da izmami *mori* Denitse divoiko | To try to seduce the maiden, Denitsa |
> | Nael se e *mori* Marko kraleviti | King Marko took the bet. |

Traditionally men accompanied their singing on a long-necked plucked lute called *tambura*, though nowadays women also play it (figure 3.11). The shape of the instrument and its name connect it to Turkey, central Asia, and even India, where the *tambura* is a drone instrument. The Pirin Mountains are home to scattered villages of Pomaks, Bulgarians who converted to Islam during the Ottoman Empire, and they most frequently played the *tambura*, though today it has become an emblem of the region and is played by Christians as well. The traditional form of the *tambura* had four strings arranged in two double courses. The player played the melody on one course and the drone on the other, creating a texture similar to the vocal style in this region (CD track 15). The modern form of the *tambura* has four double courses tuned to the same pitches as the highest-pitched strings of the guitar (E–B–G–D) and typically plays chordal accompaniments and melodies plucked on a single string.

FIGURE 3.10 *Pirin drone song, CD track 14.*

FIGURE 3.11 *Two musicians playing the modern* tambura. *(Timothy Rice, 1969)*

ACTIVITY 3.8 *Listening to CD track 15 and dancing to it* Listen for the melody and drone texture in the tambura playing on CD track 15. The first two melodies, transcribed in figure 3.12, illustrate the fact that Bulgarian instrumental tunes are often based on a constant pulsation, in this case in a meter of 7 organized 3 + 2 + 2. This meter is so associated with this region that many Bulgarians call it makedonsko horo ("Macedonian dance"). Once you can hear the basic beat pattern, form a circle holding hands and try dancing to it with the pattern of steps you learned in activity 1.1. To do this, you need to hear the rhythm as consisting of two unequal beats: 3 + 4 or 1231234. This exercise shows that the same basic steps can be danced to different meters. Notice that each version of the dance, in duple meter and in 7, has a slightly different feel.

FIGURE 3.12 Makedonsko horo *played on* tambura, *CD track 15.*

At a village dance I attended in the Pirin region in 1973, I noticed a man staring at me. Sad experience made me afraid that he was from the internal security service. He watched me dance and talk to some of the villagers for a while before finally motioning me to come over. He demanded gruffly, "Who are you?" I explained that I was an American student spending the year in Bulgaria researching traditional music. He thought about this a minute before exclaiming, "You lie!" I thought to myself, "Oh brother, here comes the accusation of spying." Instead, to my surprise he said, "You speak Bulgarian and you dance Bulgarian dances. Therefore you are a Bulgarian." Of course, I am not a Bulgarian ethnically, nor do I have any Slavic blood in my background. The music's aesthetic power and the joy of dancing to it attracted me. However, in the process of learning not just about Bulgarian culture but also how to perform aspects of it (speaking the language, dancing the dances, singing the songs, playing the tunes), I had come to resemble a Bulgarian culturally. This villager was acknowledging that it is possible to cross cultural boundaries, to enter into others' horizons of understanding, and to communicate directly with others not in a universal language but in a newly acquired particular tradition of speech, instrumental music, song, and dance. Apart from the knowledge acquired, this "becoming" through fieldwork is perhaps the most rewarding aspect of research in ethnomusicology (Rice 1997).

AFTER THE TOUR

Musical tours, real or metaphorical, are great for getting the lay of the land and learning about the variety of different musical styles in a particular culture. I am still amazed that this relatively small country possesses as much musical variety as it does. However, such surveys often leave unanswered many questions about the meaning and function of music in people's everyday lives. To answer these questions requires a period of *intensive fieldwork* in one location for a year or more. By living in one place for a year, ethnomusicologists can observe nearly all the kinds of musical events typical of that place, particularly ones tied to the cycle of seasons. I report on some of these events in chapter 4.

Making Music Yesterday and Today

The majority of Bulgarians lived in villages until the 1950s, when industrialization brought many of them to towns and cities for the first time. Before World War II, Bulgaria was primarily a rural society with an agricultural economy, and most Bulgarians farmed small plots of land surrounding their villages. Their lives, including their singing, playing, and dancing, were tied to the cycle of seasons and the rhythm of work that the seasons imposed: heavy labor in the fields during spring and summer and relatively lighter work around the house and yard during the fall and winter. During the summer they sang "harvest songs" to ease the work in the fields and in winter "sitting songs" during communal work parties at someone's home. Easter ended the Lenten fast with three days of celebratory music and dancing. Even weddings were once a seasonal ritual, planned for the fall and winter when people had finished summer field work and had prepared the foodstuffs from the harvest to host a major, often weeks-long, celebration.

The postwar processes of modernization, including urbanization, industrialization, and universal education, have changed the patterns of life and work and thus the patterns of music making in Bulgaria. Most of the old seasonal rituals have fallen by the wayside in everyday life. They have been preserved, however, in folk festivals and ensembles organized by government institutions. At festivals, for example, villagers reenact rituals to remind themselves and their audiences of the roots of their traditions. Similarly, a singer will come out onstage and announce that she is going to sing a song once sung at communal autumn gatherings of women to shuck the harvested corn, embroider a blouse, or spin wool into yarn for clothing (figure 4.1).

Old village songs, instrumental music, and dances are also heard in the mass media: radio, television, sound recordings, and videos. In these modern recordings, the song or dance or instrumental tune is almost always labeled by its old and now largely extinct use in village life before World War II. Thus modern performances have names like "sum-

FIGURE 4.1 *A woman spinning yarn.* *(Timothy Rice, 1969)*

mer dance," "Christmas song," "harvest song," and so forth. In this way the old uses and contexts for music in village life continue to live on in the modern names of what ethnomusicologists call *genres* or types of music. In peoples' imaginations, these genre names link modern performances to the old contexts that spawned the genres in the first place.

In order to understand modern performances of traditional music and the kinds of cultural and personal meanings they have for people today, I have spent a lot of time talking to people over fifty years old about their memories of music making before World War II. Here is a normative reconstruction of how musical life in a typical Bulgarian village would have been structured around the prewar agricultural and

religious calendar. This life, made more pleasant and colorful by cal-
endrical rituals, created the genres of Bulgarian instrumental music,
song, and dance heard today at folk festivals, on the radio, and in
recordings.

KOLEDA

The Bulgarian calendar of work and ritual music began at Christmas
with a tradition of house visits that involve singing, a custom related
to what Americans know as Christmas caroling. In fact, Christmas caroling has its roots in pagan fertility rituals similar to those performed
in Bulgaria, where the ritual is called *koleda* and the songs associated
with it are called *koledarski pesni* (*koleda* songs). In the month before
Christmas the boys and young men of the village gathered in groups
of a dozen or so and rehearsed a set of about twenty *koledarski pesni*. On
Christmas Eve the boys processed from house to house, often accompanied by a *gaida* player, to sing a few songs at each house. The song
texts contain good wishes for a successful year. To the head of the house
they might have sung a song wishing him a bountiful crop and many
newborn herd animals (cattle, sheep, goats), to a new bride in the house
a song wishing her a baby in the coming year, and to a girl of marriageable age a song wishing her luck in finding a husband. In exchange
for their singing, the singers received gifts of bread, wine, and meat,
and the next day they held a celebratory banquet. The whole evening
was full of noise and fun, and everyone waited excitedly for a visit from
the carolers (*koledari*).

Musically the *koleda* songs are typically sung by men in unison and
in some form of additive meter (CD track 16). Songs in meters of 5 are
especially common. These are counted 12123, 12123 or short-long, short-
long (figure 4.2).

So - bra - li sa tri de - li - ya

ta - zi gra - da Drya - no - pol - ska

FIGURE 4.2 Koleda *song, CD track 16.*

ACTIVITY 4.1 *Listening to and singing the* koleda *song on CD track 16*
Listen to the koleda *song on CD track 16, a song of plenty sung by men. Follow the transcription in figure 4.2. Divide into two equal-sized groups, as these men do, and sing the song antiphonally, that is, one group alternating with the other. Notice that each group begins on the last two syllables of the other group's verse so that they overlap and sing together for two beats. In that way, there is no pause in their singing. Try to emulate the exact way the two groups alternate and overlap.*

Sobrale sa tri deliya	Three bold youths gathered
V tazi grada Dryanopolska	In the town of Dryanopolska (refrain after each line)
Snoshti vecher na mehnata	Last evening in the tavern
Ta se hvalyat koi e yunak	And bragged about who was the best.
Provikna se pŭrvi deliya	The first bold youth cried out:
Ya sŭm yunak nad yunache	"I am the champion of champions.
Ya se imam trista kela	I have three hundred kilos,
Trista kela byalo vino	Three hundred kilos of white wine."

KUKEROVDEN

In February or March, before the Christian season of Lent, which requires a forty-day period of fasting, quiet, and reflection on the coming crucifixion and resurrection of Christ, many cultures hold a last, wild, blow-out celebration called carnival in English (and famous as Mardi Gras in New Orleans). In Bulgaria this carnival is called *kukerovden* (the day of the masqueraders or *kukeri*), and it is linked to the plowing and planting of the fields in early spring. Like *koleda*, *kukerovden* is structured around house visits. On this occasion the men of the village act out, rather than sing, their good wishes for fertility by ritually seeding the yard of each homeowner. Dressed in fantastic masks, animal skins, and large cowbells (symbolizing seeds) tied around their waists, the men go from house to house accompanied by the *gaida* and the jangling sound of the bells tied around their waists (CD track 17). In some regions they wear a tall, conical hat—a phallic symbol—and act out the ritual insemination by jerking their heads from back to front, tossing their hats onto the ground (figure 4,3). The dramatic music mixes the *gaida*'s melody and drone with the loud sound of the bells. On the road between houses, the *gaidar* plays a nonmetrical melody as the *kukeri* walk from house to house. Once in the yard, the men perform a simple *pravo horo* and *rŭchenitsa* to the *gaida*'s accompaniment.

ACTIVITY 4.2 *Listening to CD track 17*
Listen to CD track 17, a recording of kukers' *melodies played on the* gaida *to the accompaniment of the jangling bells of the* kukeri. *The first one is a version of* pravo horo, *called in this instance* kukersko horo. *The* gaidar *then changes to a nonmetrical melody, a* rŭchenitsa, *and a nonmetrical melody.*

FIGURE 4.3 Kukeri *with bells. Balkanton BHA 1045.*

EASTER DANCES

During Lent the villagers traditionally didn't dance or sing songs but remained quiet, except for some games and game-songs that were allowed for children and youth, games similar to "London Bridge Is Falling Down." But on Easter Sunday (called *velikden*, "great day") after church the village erupted in three days of celebration with dancing in the village square. Villages brought brightly decorated Easter eggs to the dancing square and cracked them with their friends in a friendly competition to see whose egg would last longest. Many of the dances were accompanied by women singing hopeful love songs whose textual imagery was often linked to the greening and flowering of nature in spring. One of my favorite Easter dance songs is from the southeastern region of Thrace and traditionally was sung antiphonally by two groups of girls in a meter of 7 counted 1212123 (CD track 18). It tells the story of Stoyan, a boy who tells his girlfriend, Dŭrgana, that recruiters for service in a faraway place have come. They argue about whether he should go and, if he does, whether she should come with him, he to play his flute and she to sing songs.

ACTIVITY 4.3 *Listening to and singing the Easter song on CD track 18*
Listen to and learn to sing the Easter dance song on CD track 18. You can study it in figure 4.4. You may find it helpful to clap on the main beats (the one's) of the meter: 7 = 2 + 2 + 3 = 1212123. Note the slight differences in the melody from verse to verse.

Dŭrgana hodi za voda	Dŭrgana went for water
A Stuyan ide ot niva	And Stoyan came from the fields.
Stuyan Dŭrgani dumashe	Stoyan said to Dŭrgana:
Lyube Dŭrgano Dŭrgano	"My love, Dŭrgana, Dŭrgana
Kakvi se konye razhozhdat	What horses they are parading
Iz vashte lyubimi dvorove	Around your beloved yards,
Vse beli konye Dŭrgano	All white horses, Dŭrgana,
Vse koprineni chuluve	All with silk blankets
I pozlateni yulari	And with golden reins."

Dŭr - ga - na   o - di za   vo - da

a Stu - yan i - de   ot   ni - va.

FIGURE 4.4   *Easter dance song from Thrace, CD track 18.*

HARVEST SONGS

During the heavy field work of summer, women sang songs to lighten the work and to entertain themselves during rest periods. Unlike many African and African American work songs, most of them are nonmetrical and don't match the rhythm of the work. Some of the most interesting field work songs are harvest songs (*zhŭtvarski pesni*) from the Shop region, sung in drone-based, two-part polyphony (CD track 19). The song texts mainly concern the specific activities of the day and the emotions and fatigue associated with them: walking to the fields, the heat at noon, the cooling breezes at the end of the day, and walking home from the fields.

ACTIVITY 4.4   *Listening to CD track 19*
Listen to CD track 19, a harvest song from the Shop region. Notice its nonmetrical quality and listen for the "cries" during and at the end of each verse, a feature of the singing style of this region. In this song the singers complain that the sun is rising earlier each day, scorching the fields—and by implication them.

DANCES AT VILLAGE FAIRS

The Bulgarian musical calendar was also defined by village fairs (called *sŭbori*, "gatherings"), held on the saint's day of the village church. Village fairs during the summer offered respite from field work and provided one of the most important contexts for dancing and its accompanying music. The generic term for these dances, danced by a circle of dancers holding hands or the belts or shoulders of their neighbors, is *horo*. The word comes from a Greek root related to the English word "chorus," meaning a group of people acting together.

Dance music has a similar structure in all meters and all over the country. The instrumentalists play a suite of melodies, each typically four or eight measures long. They play each melody two times to create a form that might be written like this: AA BB CC DD EE, and so on. When they run out of melodies they all know, the instrumentalists either return to A or they each, in no prescribed order, take a solo. Typically the solos are structured as a string of repeated melodies (say, FF GG HH, and so on) that the soloist either improvises on the spot or draws from a repertoire of tunes he has worked out in advance. The actual form at any given performance is basically improvised by the musicians from a stock of tunes they all know plus solos that fit well on each individual instrument.

ACTIVITY 4.5 *Listening to instrumental dance music on the CD*
On the CD, small ensembles or soloists play instrumental dance music on many tracks. Listen attentively to track 9. Follow the guide to its form below. Listen to tracks 1, 2, 5, 9, 10, 11, and 15. If you are ambitious, you might try to apply this kind of formal analysis to these other dance music recordings.

Form of *shopska rŭchenitsa* on CD track 9

gaida solo:	AABB
kaval solo:	4-measure transition, CCDD
gŭdulka solo	EEF
full ensemble	GF(*gŭdulka* solo)GHH

AUTUMN HOUSEWORK

In the fall and winter, after the crops were harvested and processed for winter storage, girls gathered with female friends and relatives in their homes to make clothing, sing songs, and socialize. These events, called *sedyanki* ("sittings"), transformed spinning, weaving, knitting, sewing, and embroidering into pleasant social occasions. Young women of marriageable age made their trousseaux and sang love songs in anticipation of their wedding day. *Sedyanki* also provided occasions for courting if the host's mother allowed boys to attend. They would usually arrive late in the evening, bring some musical instruments, and dance with the girls.

Musically *sedyanka* songs (*sedenkarski pesni*) are among the most melodious in the Bulgarian song repertoire. They are often highly ornamented and nonmetrical, giving the singers an opportunity to show off their vocal technique (CD track 12). The texts invoked the worsening weather as a metaphor for the hardships of married life, warning girls of difficult men and marriages and the potential for cruel mistreatment by their future mothers-in-law. Their somber mood is matched by the nonmetrical tunes. Other *sedyanka* songs are metrical and light-hearted (CD track 20). The words describe a romantic interaction between a boy and girl, who are named in the song. The singers change the names to match those present at the *sedyanka*, in the process teasing friends who seem to have an interest in one another—or who clearly do not!

ACTIVITY 4.6 *Listening, singing, and dancing to CD track 20*
Listen to CD track 20, a sedenkarska pesen *("sitting song"). This song combines a metrical dance tune with a typically somber* sedyanka *theme in the lyrics. Like the* koleda *song, it is sung antiphonally by two groups of singers, but the two groups do not overlap. Try singing the song, using the transcription in figure 4.5. After you are comfortable singing the song, try singing it while dancing* pravo horo.

Ganka na reka peryashe	Ganka laundered at the river
Ganke le kazŭm Ganke le	Ganka, beautiful Ganka (refrain)
Na reka na belyankata	At the river, at the washing place.
Ot tam ovcharche minava	A shepherd boy passed by there
To se na Ganka dumashe	And he said to Ganka:
Te chula le si Ganke le	"Have you heard, Ganka,
Temna e gŭrmezh gŭrmyalo	It got dark and thunder struck.
Gŭrmyalo dŭzhd ne valyalo	It thundered but rain didn't fall.
Trima ovcharya otdave	Three shepherds were killed.
Pŭrviya tvoya bratovched	The first was your cousin.
Vtoriya tvoya pobratim	The second was your close friend.
Tretiya tvoya lyubove	The third was your lover."

Gan - ka   na   re - ka   per - ya - she

Gan - ke   le   kaz - ŭm   Gan - ke   le

FIGURE 4.5   Sedyanka *song, CD track 20.*

WHY ARE THESE TRADITIONS STILL PERFORMED AT THE BEGINNING OF THE TWENTY-FIRST CENTURY?

Though many of the traditional contexts for Bulgarian music have died out, the music continues to be performed today for at least three reasons. First, modernization in all its forms (industrialization, urbanization, universal education, mass media) arrived relatively late in Bulgaria, after World War II. That means that older people living today grew up in villages before the war and remember the old songs, tunes, dances, and customs and have passed them on to their children and grandchildren. Second, after World War II the communist government actively supported traditional forms of instrumental music, song, and dance as part of their nationalistic and ideological agenda. They organized new contexts such as concerts, festivals, and patriotic holidays for the performance of this music, and they provided previously unknown monetary rewards, such as salaries for professional instrumentalists, singers, and dancers. This support made it worthwhile for people to learn and perform these old traditions. Third, traditional music, especially at weddings but occasionally at social gatherings in people's homes, continues to play a central role in many people's lives. Chapter 5 examines the new meanings and new contexts that arose for Bulgarian village music in the communist period from 1944 to 1989.

Music and Politics

In the summer of 1988 I accompanied two musician friends of mine—Ivan Varimezov and his wife, Tzvetanka Varimezova—to one of their performances (Rice 1994: 275–85). Ivan plays the *gaida* and was at that time the director of the orchestra of a professional ensemble of folk instrumentalists, singers, and dancers from the town of Pazardzhik in the westernmost corner of Thrace. Tzvetanka, an outstanding singer in the local style, was the ensemble's choir director. Both had been trained at the same high school and university-level conservatory where Maria Stoyanova had studied. At the schools they had learned to read musical notation and harmonize and arrange traditional melodies. The ensemble was one of sixteen professional "folk ensembles" located in major cities and towns in Bulgaria (Buchanan 1991: 661–62). I drove with them on a Saturday afternoon to a village near Pazardzhik where they were scheduled to give a concert in the central square.

A PERFORMANCE BY A
PROFESSIONAL ENSEMBLE

When we arrived, the street beside the square was lined with vendors of plastic and wooden trinkets, embroidered cloth, and cotton candy. The ensemble's performance was part of a village fair, organized by the village council (*sŭvet*), an institution run by the Communist Party. A sound system with two microphones had been set up on the square in front of the council building. Between the steps of the building and the square stood the national flags of Bulgaria and the Soviet Union, signaling the patriotic and political significance of the event. Villagers, looking rather tired and sunburned—the men dressed in the ubiquitous blue-and-gray pants and jackets of working people—had begun to gather in a large semicircle around the square as the ensemble members made their way into the council building to change into their performing costumes.

The costumes were stylized replicas of traditional village clothing from before World War II. The male instrumentalists wore baggy brown wool pants held in place by a broad swath of cloth and a leather belt at the waist. Their white shirts were embroidered in red geometric patterns down the front and along the outside of the arms. Some wore a vest over their shirts, and each man wore a black wool cap about four inches high. The female singers wore colorfully knitted stockings, wool dresses with an apron over them, and embroidered blouses with a vest or jacket over them. The jackets and dresses were decorated with strands of thread twisted into a thin rope. Some of the women wore jewelry made of gold coins to further adorn their costumes, and some wore flowers in their hair or a scarf or traditional hat. The dancers' costumes were similar, though they changed their outfits as they performed dances from the different musical regions of Bulgaria (figure 5.1).

Arranged Choral Music. The ensemble's performance began with the choir. The group of twelve women entered the square by coming

FIGURE 5.1 *A professional folk ensemble.* *(Balkanton BHA 1321)*

down the steps of the village council building. Forming a line at the two microphones, they sang an arrangement of a traditional song for unaccompanied choir. In their arrangement, the harmonies of European classical music had replaced the solo, unison (or octave) singing of Thrace and the Rhodopes and the drone-based traditional polyphony of the Shop and Pirin regions. They sang instead in a three-part, chordal, homophonic style quite foreign to traditional village practice. They didn't sound like a classical choir, however, because they preserved some elements of traditional practice. Their voice quality was close to the focused sound of traditional village style, giving the group a special tone quality that was unmistakably Bulgarian. They sang village-style ornaments, another musical reference to tradition. One of the parts was close to a drone, which had the effect of creating harmonies that evoked the "dissonance" of traditional drone-based Shop and Pirin singing (CD track 21). The song itself used traditional melodies and rhythms of Bulgarian village singing, further enhancing the impression that this could only be a certain kind of Bulgarian music, not merely classical European music with a Bulgarian tinge. After their song, they exited back up the stairs of the council building as the instrumentalists entered.

ACTIVITY 5.1 *Listening to CD track 21*
Listen to CD track 21, a recording of an arranged folk song sung by the Pazardzhik ensemble choir at a village fair in 1988. Listen for the homophonic texture and the slight "dissonance" of the harmonies.

Arranged Instrumental Music. As the choir exited, the instrumental ensemble came down the steps and formed a line at the microphones. Instead of a single soloist or a small ensemble of three or four instruments, as had been traditional in the prewar era, the nine instrumentalists formed an orchestra consisting of one *kaval*, one *gaida*, three *gŭdulkas*, a string bass in the shape of a *gŭdulka*, two *tamburas*, and a *tŭpan*.

They played a suite of tunes in different meters (CD track 22). The suite is a new form designed for concert presentation. Traditionally instrumentalists played one dance in one meter, often for a rather long time, stopped, and started up a new dance, often at the dancers' request. Arrangers of folk music used the suite form to create musical variety and hold the attention of a passive, listening audience. The musicians began with some tunes for *pravo horo*, then slowed down and launched into some tunes in perhaps the longest Bulgarian additive meter, 33 pulses to a phrase (notated as 15 + 18 in figure 5.2). Also new to the tradition were chords played on the *tamburas* and *gŭdulkas* and bass *gŭdulka* and countermelodies played by the *gŭdulkas* simultaneously with the main melody. These devices added musical interest for listeners who cared about such things. I doubt whether the assembled villagers did, as they looked on without much enthusiasm and applauded politely at the end. Nonetheless, for many educated, urban listeners, such ensembles create an attractive sound that melds together traditional and modern ways of making music.

> **ACTIVITY 5.2** *Listening to CD track 22*
> Listen to CD track 22, a recording of the suite of instrumental tunes performed by the Pazardzhik ensemble. Listen for the chords and countermelodies in the first section, pravo horo. The meter of the second section, called smeseno horo ("mixed dance"), is made up of three traditional meters strung together: 15 + 9 + 9 to form a single phrase of 33 pulses, subdivided as follows: 2 + 2 + 2 + 2 + 3 + 2 + 2/2 + 2 + 2 + 3/2 + 3 + 2 + 2. The second phrase, the B phrase, is shortened to include just the last two sections of nine beats each for a meter of 18. Follow this along aurally while looking at the notation of the melody in figure 5.2.

FIGURE 5.2 *Tunes in 33 and 18 meters, CD track 22.*

Choreographed Dancing. After the instrumental tune, the male and female dancers of the company came down the steps of the council building, past the Bulgarian and Soviet flags, and performed a series of dances from the Thracian and Shop regions of the country. Instead of the traditional open-circle formation, they altered the basic formal principles of Bulgarian dance in ways at least as profound as the modern musical arrangements altered traditional musical practice. The professional ensembles used choreographers trained in some of the elements of classical ballet to break up the circle and vary the repetitive dance pattern to create interest for a viewing audience. Typically pairs and short lines of dancers faced the audience and rarely moved in a circle, to avoid turning their backs toward the audience. These short lines moved swiftly across the "stage" formed by the open space in the village square. The dancers were enormously skilled, young, and vibrant, their footwork alternately graceful and intense. The audience seemed to appreciate the dancing more than the concert of choral and instrumental music, but many were already looking forward to their chance to dance to the band of wedding instrumentalists setting up on the porch of the council building.

Political Symbolism. Comparing this event to prewar musical life described in the previous chapter makes it clear that Bulgarian traditional music changed dramatically in the second half of the twentieth century. Postwar musical events functioned as government-sponsored entertainment and political symbol. The performance was a microcosm and particular instance of larger political and ideological forces at work in Bulgaria from 1944 to 1989. For some especially skilled instrumentalists, singers, and dancers, what had been primarily a pastime before World War II became a profession. Music, song, and dance, which had been a communal and community activity with the participation of all according to certain gender rules, became a performing art with a sharp split between performers and audience. What had been an important context in which to act out social relations had become a symbol of the Communist Party, the nation, and submission to Soviet domination in cultural, political, and economic matters. When and why and how this happened is the subject of the next section (see also Buchanan 1991, 1995, 1996; Rice 1994: 169–233, 1996; Silverman 1982, 1983).

MODERNIZATION AND A NEW IDEOLOGY COME TO BULGARIA

On 9 September 1944, less than a year before the end of World War II, Bulgarian communists declared a victory over German fascism and a victory for the Communist Party as the leading state institution. Over the next ten to fifteen years the party consolidated its power, nationalized and collectivized private farmland, created a more powerful industrial economy, and improved educational opportunities for all its citizens.

These changes profoundly affected musical life, tied as it was to farm life in villages. Party ideology, for example, strongly discouraged religious practices. Because churches could no longer be the center of social life on saints' days, and because party officials sometimes intervened to put a stop to fertility and other magical rituals on the grounds that they were "superstitious," many of the most important contexts and excuses for making music disappeared—except in memory. Many young people in their teens or early twenties left their villages to pursue a high school education or a better job in a nearby town. In doing so, they lost touch with the home environment that nurtured traditional music learning and as a result often failed to learn the village repertoire of songs, dances, and instrumental tunes.

At the same time that the forces of ideology and modernization seemed arrayed against traditional music and dance practices, the Communist Party created new institutions and ideas that helped them to flourish in new contexts and new forms. One new idea was that rural music, as an expression of the common man (the proletariat), could be a useful symbol of the new society. As a consequence of this belief, party functionaries invented new institutions to support traditional rural music and place it at the center of national attention and consciousness.

A second new idea suggested that centralized, state support of the arts could be used to create the "new man" that would be necessary to "build communism." For this reason, the communist government supported arts education as strongly as it did education in the sciences and literature. The government, in other words, understood the power of art, especially the performing arts, to symbolically represent a world in an attractive manner full of positive feelings. The world they wanted to represent was not the dreary present with its poverty and struggle—the world of the gray-and-blue-clad workers in the village near Pazardzhik. Rather, it was the bright, happy, prosperous, progressive world of the future promised by communism. The party couldn't create that world in reality because of nearly insurmountable economic problems (and some would say a flawed theory of how to do it), but they could model it ideologically in art, particularly music and dance.

Communist ideology is based on nineteenth-century ideas about the evolution and progress of humankind through stages from the primitive to the civilized. For this reason, all types of art flourished under the patronage of the Bulgarian government during the communist period. New symphony orchestras, opera and ballet companies, and classical music festivals were founded in the major cities. From the early days of the Soviet Union, founded in 1917, and through most of the twentieth century, communist governments in eastern Europe suppressed the possible symbolic association of classical music with the aristocratic and bourgeois classes that patronized it. Instead, they focused on classical music as a symbol of the greatest achievements of Western civilization, ignoring ironically the social classes and economic conditions that fostered that music.

Traditional, rural music was also a symbolic double-edged sword. It was clearly useful as a powerful symbol of national identity and had a great deal of significance and emotional resonance for villagers and workers who migrated to the cities and towns from villages. It was, however, also problematically associated with the poverty and exploitation of those classes by the precommunist economic and social systems.

The solution to the problem and the reconciliation of the double and opposite meanings of both classical and traditional music was to turn one into the other, that is, to imbue traditional music with the aesthetic forms and values and positive symbolic meanings of classical music. This was accomplished by using the techniques of classical music to "arrange" the music—a word with the added implication in Bulgarian of "improving" the music (Buchanan 1991). These techniques include all the devices we observed in the village near Pazardzhik: adding chordal accompaniments and countermelodies to previously unaccompanied melodies; singing in choruses instead of solos or duets; playing in orchestras rather than solo or in small bands; dressing up in old-fashioned costumes for performances; and creating performance situations with a sharp split between the active performers and their passive audience. Other aspects of classical music applied to traditional music included training instrumentalists in musical notation, theory, and composition and allowing them to enter the economic system as full-time professional instrumentalists. (There are always exceptions to such strong generalizations, including Rom instrumentalists who eked out a meager living as professional instrumentalists before World War II.) All of these things were new and foreign to the traditional, prewar practice of Bulgarian village music.

NEW INSTITUTIONS FOR THE NEW FOLK MUSIC

These changes didn't just happen by ideological fiat. They required new institutions, created and backed financially by the government. One of the first things the government did, in 1951, was to invite a well-known classical composer named Phillip Koutev to organize a "State Ensemble of Folk Song and Dance" modeled on similar companies in the Soviet Union (figure 5.3). Koutev and other Bulgarian composers had already been arranging and composing Bulgarian folk songs for classically trained choirs in Sofia before the war, but Koutev understood that such an ensemble would have to be truer to village models than classical ensembles are. So, instead of hiring classically trained instrumentalists and singers, he arranged auditions around the country to find the best village singers, dancers, and instrumentalists. He sent dance specialists to the Soviet Union to learn how to choreograph village dances for presentation on the stage, and he created an orchestra of village instruments and a choir of village singers on the Soviet model that preserved the tone quality of traditional music while dressing it up in new, urbane clothing.

FIGURE 5.3   *Phillip Koutev with his singers.*   *(Balkanton BHA 1103)*

What became known as the "Koutev ensemble" made a positive impression both internally and abroad in the 1950s and 1960s. It was touring to great success in the United States, for example, when President John F. Kennedy was assassinated in 1963. In 1965 Nonesuch Records released a recording of the ensemble that was influential in the American folk music scene of the 1960s. It was one of the records that got me interested in Bulgarian music. In 1954 a similar orchestra and choir were formed at the national radio station, Radio Sofia. For the next forty years, this kind of "cultivated folk music" filled the airwaves and was produced by the national record company, Balkanton. Eventually nearly every major town had its own professional folk ensemble.

These new ensembles needed good instrumentalists, singers, and dancers. In 1967 a high school to train them was founded, followed by a second one in 1972. A postsecondary "pedagogical institute" continued the training of the high school graduates and prepared them to direct provincial professional ensembles and the many amateur groups that had sprung up in villages all over the country.

Amateur village groups were also part of the new ideological plan for society. They flourished under the direction of an arm of a governmental organization devoted to "artistic amateurism." Participating in such groups was not just an artistic act but also a political act, if a rather benign one. Rewards included travel around the region and country to folk festivals. The best groups were invited to international festivals in nearby countries, providing one of the few opportunities for travel abroad during the communist era.

These village groups typically didn't employ the same elaborate arrangements and choreographies as the professional ensembles. They stuck closer to traditional practices. They still required, however, some supervision and direction, either from schoolteachers trained in the "artistic amateurism" organization or graduates of the high schools for folk music. The directors coached the ensembles in such things as intonation, costuming, choice of repertoire, and stage entrances and exits.

CULTIVATED FOLK MUSIC

A more detailed examination of the way Phillip Koutev and those who followed after him treated Bulgarian traditional music helps to understand how they sought to make "cultivated folk music" symbolically appropriate to the new state and aesthetically pleasing to an audience with a higher degree of education than the prewar, rural performers of folk music. Examining the structures of this new music helps make clear the art that went into these arrangements and compositions.

One of Koutev's most famous and effective choral compositions is a song called "Polegnala e Todora" (Todora was taking a nap). Koutev began with a traditional song tune in four measures in a meter of 11 (2 + 2 + 3 + 2 + 2), but everything else about the piece is composed. First he added a second melody of four measures to lengthen the song's form. Then his wife, Maria Kouteva, composed a new text on a folk theme. The text tells of a girl who lies down to rest in the shade of a tree, but she becomes annoyed when falling leaves interrupt her dreams of a boyfriend (CD track 23). Koutev created a three-part choral score for the original melody and set his composed melody for a quartet of soloists (figure 5.4). In the first section, Koutev divided the choir into two groups so they could sing antiphonally, a common traditional performance practice. The accompanying parts move in the same rhythm as the melody to create a smooth homophonic texture that emphasizes the melody and words. The harmonies are based on the most basic chords of European classical music. In the four-part section Koutev injected a bit of the traditional texture of village singing by holding one part as close as possible to a drone. Finally, the traditional elements were cemented in place by the singers' throaty vocal quality and ornamentation, recorded in the notation with grace notes sung right on the beat before moving on to the main melody note.

ACTIVITY 5.3 *Listening to and singing the song on CD track 23 Listen to CD track 23, Phillip Koutev's composition "Polegnala e Todora," while following the notation in figure 5.4. In the B section, find the part closest to a drone. Listen for the grace notes. Organize a group and try singing the song. The text concerns a girl dreaming of becoming engaged. Each line of text is followed by a refrain, and the line plus refrain are each sung twice. Notice that when sung, Todora is pronounced Tudora.*

Polegnala e Todora	Todora was taking a nap
moma Todoro Todoro	O maiden Todora, Todora (refrain)
Pod dŭrvo, pod maslinovo	Underneath a tree, an olive tree.
Poveya vetrets, gornenets.	A wind blew, a north wind.
Otkŭrshi klonka maslina,	It snapped off an olive branch,
Che si Todora sŭbudi	So that Todora woke up.
A tya mu se lyuto sŭrdi:	And she angrily scolded it:
Vetre le nenaveyniko,	"Unwanted wind,
Sega li nayde da veesh?	Why now did you decide to blow?

Sladka si sŭnya sŭnuvah,	I was dreaming a sweet dream,
Che mi doshlo pŭrvo libe	That my first love had come,
I doneslo pŭstra kitka,	And brought me a colorful bouquet,
I doneslo pŭstra kitka,	And brought me a colorful bouquet,
A na kitka zlaten prŭsten.	And on the bouquet a gold [wedding] ring."

FIGURE 5.4 *"Polegnala e Todora" by Phillip Koutev, CD track 23.* (Used by kind permission of Rykomusic Inc.)

Arrangements of instrumental dance music used the same classical music aesthetic applied to the newly created orchestra of traditional instruments. One such arrangement, *krivo plovdivsko horo* (Crooked Dance from the Plovdiv Region), is in a meter of 13 organized 2 + 2 + 2 + 3 + 2 + 2 (CD track 24). Like so many of these arrangements, it harkens back to traditional practice by featuring a soloist, in this case the famous *kaval* player Nikola Ganchev, who played with the Koutev ensemble. The arrangement is also traditionally structured into a series of tunes, each played twice. New to the tradition are harmonies and accompaniments added to create musical interest for listeners rather than dancers. Each new tune is usually marked by a change in the accompaniment. Some of the compositional devices include (1) bass note and chord in alternation; (2) block chords punching out the rhythm with pauses for emphasis; (3) a contrast between full orchestra and thinner textures with just the *tamburas* plucking; and (4) chords plus countermelodies.

ACTIVITY 5.4 *Listening to CD track 24*
Listen to CD track 24, an arrangement of krivo plovdivsko
horo. *Your first task is to find the basic meter (2 + 2 + 2 +
3 + 2 + 2). Then try to hear the four-measure phrases, each re-
peated once. Listen also for the accompaniment texture of each
melody, described below.*
AA   *full orchestra*
BB   kaval *solo with tamburas; on the repeat* gŭdulkas *and
       low strings enter with bass and chords*
CC   kaval *solo, bass and chords with countermelody, full or-
       chestra on repeat*
DD   kaval, *bass and chords, full orchestra in second half of
       repeat*
EE   kaval, tamburas *with bass and chords, full orchestra*
FF   kaval *and* tamburas; *bass enters on repeat*
GG   *fade out*

For most of the forty-five-year-long communist period, this style of cultivated folk music became the standard way "folk music" (*narodna muzika*, "people's music") was presented on the radio and in recordings and concerts. Many composers produced similar compositions for the growing number of professional and amateur folk orchestras and choirs. While the same basic techniques were used, the style evolved somewhat during that period (Buchanan 1991: 377–405). For example, in choral compositions composers began to experiment with a greater use of dissonance to replace the consonant harmonies that Koutev used in the early years of the communist period. This experiment with dissonance worked well at least partly because there was such a good match between the dissonant sound of modern, twentieth-century classical music and the traditional dissonance created by drone-based singing from the Shop and Pirin regions.

> **ACTIVITY 5.5** *Listening to CD track 25*
> Listen to CD track 25, a composition entitled "Zaspala e moma" (A girl fell asleep) by Stefan Dragostinov, who served as artistic director of the Koutev ensemble in the 1980s. Compare its dissonant, close harmonies to those of Koutev's in "Polegnala e Todora" on CD track 23. Which composition do you prefer, and why?

NEW MEANING FOR WEDDING MUSIC

At the same time that these musical and cultural developments were changing the artistic form, symbolic meaning, and economic value of traditional music, Bulgarians continued to marry and to need instrumentalists to play for wedding celebrations. Before World War II most weddings would have been accompanied by the villagers' own singing and playing, or they might have hired some local Roma for a small sum of money. During the communist period, with the growth of a money economy and state support of a new class of professional instrumentalists, more people could afford to hire instrumentalists—and there were more professional instrumentalists to hire. These instrumentalists were not only Roma, who had been professionals in the past, but also Bulgarians who had become professionals for state ensembles or who, as semiprofessional part-time instrumentalists, had the skills to make money in the new "grey" economy.

One of the early modernizing moves in the wedding music tradition, starting in the late nineteenth century, was the incorporation of manufactured instruments to replace traditional Bulgarian instruments. The clarinet and the accordion became the most important and widespread wedding music instruments by the mid-twentieth century in many parts of the country. In western Bulgaria, the trumpet and entire brass bands gained prominence (figure 5.5). In northern Bulgaria, the violin entered the tradition, probably owing to influence from Romania, where the instrument is commonly used. The *tŭpan* is still used, but drummers often add a cymbal to the body. Eventually an entire drum kit became common, and over time other modern instruments have been added to wedding bands, including saxophone, electric bass and guitar, and synthesizer. These last instruments require sound systems and electronic amplification, which had become a crucial element in the sound of wedding music by the late 1970s.

The structure of performances has otherwise remained traditional. For a given *horo*, the entire band plays a few tunes that they know in common and then each melodic instrument takes a solo. The main new development was that, since these modern instruments are not as limited in range as traditional ones are, the range of melodies increased

FIGURE 5.5   *A Bulgarian brass band playing at a wedding.*   (Timothy Rice, 1972)

substantially. Also, since modern instruments can play easily and chromatically in many keys, rapid changes from key to key and arpeggiated and chromatic melodies became a hallmark of wedding music (CD tracks 26, 27).

The wedding and state-supported folk music traditions developed in parallel for many years, from the 1950s through the 1970s. But in the 1980s, the last decade of the communist period, they began to diverge musically, economically, and symbolically.

The first cause of these changes was probably economic. The communist economy did not work on a supply-and-demand principle. It was, rather, a "command economy." The problem with such economies is that government-run industries typically produce too much of what people don't want and too little of what they do. In particular, consumer goods were always in short supply. As a consequence of not having much to buy, Bulgarians built up large reserves of savings. They then spent their savings on private services, such as foreign-language lessons for their children, and symbolic display, such as hiring the best, most famous instrumentalists and singers for lavish weddings, like the ones I described in chapter 1. The economic power of this private economy was so great by the 1980s that many instrumentalists in the state-supported ensembles had left or were contemplating leaving to play in the more lucrative wedding music scene. Many wedding instrumentalists had become stars, better known around the country than all but a handful of folk singers and instrumentalists. The most famous was a clarinetist named Ivo Papazov, whose recordings were released in the United States (Buchanan 1996).

Changes in the Sound of Wedding Music.   As wedding music developed under the patronage of an increasingly wealthy private economy beyond state control, instrumentalists began to expand its musical properties without the supervision of government authorities from the Ministry of Culture and the national radio and recording industries. These developments occurred in virtually every aspect of the music (Rice 1996).

First, wedding instrumentalists' and their clients' sensibilities gravitated more toward popular music than the classical aesthetic being imposed on folk music by classically trained composers. Instrumentalists pumped up the sound of the music through ever more elaborate and powerful sound systems, which they could afford to buy with all the money being thrown at them.

Second, since many of the bands played nearly every day of the week at weddings and other family celebrations (sending boys off to military service had become another popular event requiring music), their playing technique developed spectacularly. They had complete command of their instruments, and they began to play at extraordinarily fast tempos to show off their virtuosity. They also began to play more elaborate, wider-ranging improvisations, filled with syncopations, chromaticisms, and arpeggios inspired by jazz and popular music.

Third, since they worked outside government control, they were no longer bound by the nationalistic agenda associated with "folk music." Since many wedding instrumentalists were Roma, they played Rom music, especially a dance called *kyuchek*. Primarily a solo dance with rapid hip movements that resemble what Americans know as "belly dancing," to Bulgarians in the 1980s it seemed sexually suggestive and therefore either liberating or licentious, depending in part on their political point of view. Rom wedding instrumentalists also introduced what some Bulgarians called "oriental" elements into their playing such as nonmetrical improvisations over the basic beat of the dance. They also played popular hits from neighboring countries, especially Serbia, Romania, Turkey, and Greece. The freedom of their playing and their freedom from the restraints imposed on folk music helped wedding music become wildly popular during the 1980s.

ACTIVITY 5.6 *Listening to CD tracks 26 and 27*
On the audio CD, tracks 26 and 27 contain examples of wedding music from the 1980s. CD track 26, recorded by Ivo Papazov is a studio recording and, although technically brilliant, is rather restrained compared to his wildest playing at weddings. Still, it shows off some of his instrumental skills and the fast tempos, key changes, melodic arpeggiations, syncopations, and chromaticisms that characterize wedding music. CD track 27, recorded by another excellent band at a festival devoted to wedding music, captures the raw energy and the rough sound quality of live performances.

The Politics of Wedding Music. Besides the brilliance of the instrumentalists, people's increasing dissatisfaction with the communist government also contributed to the enormous popularity of wedding music. The government created problems for itself in the 1980s by instituting draconian measures against the Turks and Roma, Bulgaria's Muslim minorities (Poulton 1990, Silverman 1989). Apparently fearing that these minorities had grown so large in number that they might begin to demand cultural autonomy, the government decided to solve the problem by symbolically erasing them and their culture from the national consciousness. They did this by forcing Muslims to change their names to Christian ones or some other approved Bulgarian name. For example, Ivo Papazov had first gained fame as Ibryam Hapazov, but was required to change his name. The government apparently reasoned that without Muslim names they could no longer be identified in a census. They also banned nearly all forms of "oriental" public cultural display, including speaking Turkish, the wearing of traditional pants (*shalvari*) by women, and the playing of Rom forms of music and dance such as *kyuchek*, with its elaborate nonmetrical improvisations. One of the reasons the Roma at the wedding I described in chapter 1 were dancing *rŭchenitsa*s and not their own *kyuchek*s was precisely because of this ban on Rom cultural display. Bulgarian cultural officials began to claim that all these practices, including much of what was popular about wedding music, were "aggressively antistate."

At one level wedding music was antistate simply because it operated in an economic sphere largely beyond state control. But in the highly charged political environment in Bulgaria in the late 1980s, the musical form of wedding music also became an icon of people's hopes for freedom and a more democratic form of government. An icon is a symbolic form that possesses some of the properties of the thing it represents. Wedding music's emphasis on improvisation by individual instrumentalists, and especially forms of improvisation that broke the bounds of traditional practice, could be interpreted as an iconic representation of the individual freedom Bulgarians increasingly sought in the political arena. It also provided a new "structure of feeling" that allowed people to experience some release and relief within an otherwise repressive and restrictive society (Williams 1977: 128–35).

Furthermore, if folk music, including all its features (highly arranged, emphasis on traditional instruments, narrow-range diatonic melodies, lack of real improvisation), was by its association with government institutions an obvious symbol of the state, then wedding music, with all its contrasting features, could be interpreted as a symbol of antistate sentiments. Those features included a flexible structure that was responsive to the audience rather than completely prearranged; an emphasis on modern instruments; wide-ranging, chromatic melodies; and a preference for amplified over acoustic sound. While these features by themselves cannot be said to be iconic of anything, let alone antitotalitarian feelings, in this particular context, where they existed in striking contrast to the music patronized by the state, such features can be interpreted as expressions of the yearning for political freedom (Rice 2001).

One of the general lessons that this Bulgarian example teaches is that music can have referential meaning. The way it "means" something, however, is highly variable and linked to specific cultural, social, and performance situations. A second general lesson is that the meaning of music and musical performance can be carried in the sound of the music, not just in the texts. The song texts of wedding music remained rather traditional and nothing like the protest songs associated with many oppositional political movements around the world. Still, antigovernment sentiments were carried no less effectively and possibly even more powerfully in the musical sounds themselves.

FROM BEHAVIOR TO SYMBOL TO COMMODITY

In the second half of the twentieth century, modernization all over the world has threatened the continued existence of rural musical traditions. In Bulgaria many traditional practices nearly died owing to economic changes or were banned in the name of the new communist ideology. What helped save these traditions was the interest the state took in them for ideological reasons. Though the government transformed tradition in significant ways through arrangements and choreographies, it nonetheless created an intellectual, artistic, and economic environment that demanded *gaida*s and *kaval*s and singers and dancers who could perform in the old village manner.

Many Bulgarians' love of village music and dance, even after they moved to cities, meant that they patronized the tradition by paying musicians to play at elaborate family celebrations, particularly weddings. Thus politics, aesthetics, economics, and social behavior meshed in a particularly productive way to keep Bulgarian traditional music alive, vital, and changing to meet the needs of Bulgarians living in a vastly different world from the one in which the music had been originally created.

Through state and private patronage, this new music, which some scholars call neotraditional music, had become a kind of commodity. Instrumentalists could, in the communist economy, sell their musical labor on an increasingly lucrative mass-mediated market. State ensembles toured abroad, spreading the ideological message of the state in wonderfully pleasing theatrical forms. Some Bulgarian recordings over the years slipped into the international market for what came to be called around 1989 "world music." That process of commodification and the subsequent escape of Bulgarian music from local and national meanings is an important element in understanding many kinds of traditional music from around the world. I'll take this topic up in chapter 6.

CHAPTER 6

Bulgarian Music as World Music

In 1995 I received a phone call from Joe LoDuca, a film-and-television composer from Michigan. He said that he had been hired to write the music for a new syndicated TV series called *Xena, Warrior Princess*, and he was going to use Bulgarian music as the theme. Needless to say, I was quite surprised and asked him why. He explained that the producers had heard some recordings of Bulgarian arranged choral music, similar to those mentioned in chapter 5, released on the Nonesuch label under the title *Le mystère des voix bulgares* (The mystery of the Bulgarian voices). They thought that the powerful sound of these female voices would be a perfect sonic representation of their powerful female heroine.

He was coming to Los Angeles to record his score in a few weeks and asked if I could help him find appropriate words for the song text and a group of singers who could mimic the sound of Bulgarian choirs. As it happens, a number of songs in the Bulgarian tradition recount the exploits of female warriors. These women, called *bairaktarki* (female flag bearers), joined the guerrillas (*haiduti*) who fought against the Turks during the Ottoman period. Like all flag bearers, they were the first targets of the enemy and therefore were considered the bravest of the brave. They were drawn into battle either to be with husbands or lovers or because they had been "shamed" in some way and therefore had no future in normal village society. Something similar occurred in 1999 during the fighting in the Kosovo province of Yugoslavia when some Serbian fighters raped Albanian women, some of whom, having been thus shamed, were reported to have joined the fighting against the Serbs.

I told him that two local women's groups sang Bulgarian choral music in this style. Although there are many such groups in the United States and in other countries such as Japan and Denmark, it is almost impossible for them to capture exactly the sound of Bulgarian voices. I knew a Bulgarian woman living near Los Angeles who had been a professional singer in Bulgaria, however, and I suggested that he have her record all the parts over the American choir to capture just the right sound. Although I didn't attend the recording session, I found out later that the woman's husband, a former professional *kaval* player with the Koutev ensemble, also attended and recorded some music on the *gaida* for the soundtrack.

I could hardly wait to hear and see the result and watched with great interest when *Xena* debuted on television. The opening montage begins with an airborne shot of a rugged coastline accompanied by a nonmetrical melody on the *gaida* (CD track 28). The composer clearly had made an association between a natural scene and the sound of the bagpipe, and since bagpipes were once used in Bulgaria to ward off the boredom of shepherds in the fields, this association is close to a Bulgarian reality. As the opening changes to show scenes of Xena in various settings, a female choir sings a melody in a meter of 7 (2 + 2 + 3), the *rŭchenitsa* dance rhythm first heard in chapter 1. The melody, based on a narrow-range, three-note motive, has analogues in Bulgarian music, and the arrangement imitates the drone-like textures of some traditional and arranged singing. Obviously Joe had done his homework and captured important elements of Bulgarian music in his composition. As the show progressed, it became clear that Bulgarian female singing was used whenever Xena went into battle, creating a symbolic association between Xena's fierceness and the sound of Bulgarian women's voices singing in the style of arranged choral music. Unlike the *gaida*'s association with the natural and pastoral, which has links to Bulgarian practice, this symbolic connection between women's choral singing and violence or powerful females has little if anything to do with Bulgarian realities. It is strictly an American take on what such a powerful female sound might represent.

ACTIVITY 6.1 *Listening to CD track 28*
Listen to CD track 28, the main title music from Xena, War-rior Princess. *Listen for the* gaida *and the meter of 7 when the Bulgarian women's voices enter. If you can, watch the opening of the television show, which uses a slightly different version of this piece for its opening montage.*

BULGARIAN MUSIC HITS THE CHARTS

The use of Bulgarian music for *Xena, Warrior Princess* was the tip of an iceberg of renewed interest in "world music" that began at the end of the 1980s. More and more musicians from around the world began to issue new recordings, in the then-new audio CD format, of their own traditional music combined with elements of rock, pop, soul, jazz, and hip-hop music. They did so in part as a means of keeping their own traditions alive and fresh. American music, it seemed, had conquered the world and was coming back to America in new and fascinating forms. Many musicians in other cultures simply adopted American-derived pop styles and tried to imitate them by singing songs in English or their own language. Others merged their own traditional music with American popular styles to create new kinds of "global pop" music that at once signaled their allegiance to ancient cultural values and practices and to their own modernity.

British music promoters and media executives, realizing that they were experiencing a new musical phenomenon, met in the summer of 1987 to decide what to call this new kind of music so they could market it effectively (Taylor 1997). Old labels used in the 1960s and 1970s, such as "ethnic" and "international," had become passé, and new labels, like "world beat" and "ethno-pop," were beginning to appear. To halt this proliferation of terms, which undercut their marketing efforts, they agreed to call this new kind of fusion of traditional and popular music "world music." Soon *Billboard* magazine, which publishes music industry news and charts product sales, had introduced a new list with that name.

As a rule, most recordings of this kind of popular "world music" employ a synthesis of traditional music with the rhythms, beats, and instruments (electric guitars and basses, drum sets, synthesizers) of Western rock and pop music. One exception to this rule was the popularity on the "world music" charts of the *Le mystère* recordings heard by the producers of *Xena* that contained *a cappella* choral music on a classical music model.

First popular in Britain and then, after their release on the Nonesuch label, in the United States, volume 1 of *Le mystère* rose to the top of the new *Billboard* world music chart in 1988, and volume 2 won a Grammy for best traditional recording in 1989. Though the rock-pop influence of most "world music" productions was missing, the two recordings were popular with a new audience of European and American pop musicians and their fans. Bulgarian choirs have toured the United States almost annually since 1988, giving sold-out performances in major concert halls around the country. At a concert I attended of a Bulgarian choir in Los Angeles in 1990, the audience included such pop icons as David Crosby and Frank Zappa. After a concert in 1998, Stevie Wonder sang and played piano for the enraptured choir.

Something about the music's combination of familiar harmonies, relatively simple song forms, unique vocal quality, and vocal ornamentation had an enormous appeal in this new market for world music. The choirs sang Koutev's compositions from the 1950s as well as some of the more modern compositions that used more dissonant techniques (CD tracks 21, 23, 25). To judge from audience applause, some of the most modern arrangements made the biggest impression.

ACTIVITY 6.2   *Listening to* Le mystère des voix bulgares
Find a volume of the recordings called Le mystère des voix bulgares *(Nonesuch 79165, 79201; Polygram/Fontana 846 626) and listen to a sampling of the recordings. Can you distinguish between the compositions with more consonant harmonies and those with more dissonant harmonies? Try to identify some songs that employ traditional techniques of solo and drone-based singing.*

The popularity of this Bulgarian singing outside Bulgaria depends, in the first instance, on its reception as a work of art, that is, on a positive evaluation of its sounds and the interpretation of it as "good music." After that, however, people often seek some kind of meaning in music. Since Bulgaria is relatively unknown in the United States, relating the music to Bulgaria and its cultural traditions was not very likely.

Instead, foreign listeners attributed at least three meanings to this music, meanings that had little or nothing to do with the social and political context in which it was produced. First, some people interpreted these recordings as "authentic" folk music. These recordings seemed to awaken in some Americans a yearning for ancient, traditional, premodern experiences that have been eclipsed by modernity. Second, a number of newspaper reviewers interpreted the music as "out of this world" in a double sense, as something so terrific it could only come from the cosmos. Perhaps because Bulgaria is nowhere in Americans' earthly cultural imagination, it seemed possible to imagine that it must have come from outer space, a kind of music of the spheres. Third, the association of a powerful female vocal sound with a new kind of powerful femininity was part of the attraction of this music for many women, as evidenced in *Xena, Warrior Princess* but also in the existence of many American women's choirs devoted to replicating its sounds.

These examples demonstrate the more general principle that meanings attached to music are not inherent in its sound. They are added to or associated with the music. In this fashion, music's meaning can change over time and as it moves from place to place. Even in a given time and place, there often is not as much agreement about the meaning of a musical piece or performance as there usually is about the meaning of a word or a speech utterance; however, that doesn't mean that music has no meaning. On the contrary, it means that music is capable of bearing a plethora of different and often conflicting meanings. Indeed, the ability to freely change and invent new meanings for music is an important source of its cultural, social, and political power.

In the case of Bulgarian music in the 1980s and 1990s, the meanings Americans imputed to it were American meanings. They often did not correspond to the meanings Bulgarians attributed to it. But does that matter? In some sense, no. That is, for Bulgarian music to be as popular as it has been outside Bulgaria, it has to be made meaningful in a world rather different from the one in which it originated. On the other hand, these new meanings reveal more about our own culture than about Bulgarian culture. When interpretations take on an element of parody, as they did in an album with the title *From Bulgaria with Love*, then one has to wonder about the motivation and ethics of those who created these new meanings (Buchanan 1997).

Frequently only ethnomusicologists and students of ethnomusicology go beyond these American meanings to recover something of the meaning the music has for the people who produce it. They do so through a process called musical ethnography, which, as mentioned in chapter 3, requires periods of residence in the society itself. Still, even in the absence of such culturally specific explanations, Americans thoroughly enjoy Bulgarian music and many other kinds of "world music" as forms of artistic expression.

APPROPRIATING BULGARIAN MUSIC

Foreigners' interest in Bulgarian traditional music predates the popular interest in *Le mystère des voix bulgares* by many decades. Bulgarian music has also enthralled classical and jazz composers, as well as a community of international folk dancers and choral singers. The additive meters of Bulgarian traditional music, so unusual in European and American classical and popular music, caught the attention of the famous Hungarian composer Béla Bartók (1881–1945) in the 1920s (Rice 2000). In addition to being a composer, Bartók was also an important folk song collector and researcher and kept up with research on traditional music throughout eastern Europe, the Middle East, and north Africa. Bartók wrote scholarly articles about what he called "Bulgarian rhythms" and made them available to a wider public by incorporating them into his own classical compositions, including the suite "Six Dances in Bulgarian Rhythms," part of a six-volume set of graded compositions for piano students called *Mikrokosmos*.

ACTIVITY 6.3 *Listening to Béla Bartók's "Six Dances in Bulgarian Rhythms"*
Find a recording of Bartók's "Six Dances in Bulgarian Rhythms" from volume 6 of Mikrokosmos *and, if you can read musical notation, compare it to the score. Which Bulgarian meters did he use? Try counting them.*

During the 1960s, disaffected American youth turned famously to sex, drugs, and rock 'n' roll as they protested national policy in Vietnam and supported the civil rights movement. A fascination with world music as an alternative to American popular culture also characterized this period, and Bulgarian music joined Latin, Brazilian, African, and Indian music in the musical mix. Many jazz and rock musicians appropriated the melodic modes, rhythms, and instruments of these traditions for use in their own creations. A well-known California jazz band leader named Don Ellis used Bulgarian and Indian additive meters in a number of compositions, including an arrangement entitled "Bulgarian Bulge" (CD track 29). Ellis's pianist, Milcho Leviev, a Bulgarian who had fled the country during the communist period, provided the "head" of the piece, a tune Bulgarian musicians call *smeseno horo* ("mixed dance"). In a meter of 33 (2 + 2 + 2 + 2 + 3 + 2 + 2/2 + 2 + 2 + 3/2 + 3 + 2 + 2), it is the same melody played by the Pazardzhik ensemble on CD track 22 and transcribed in figure 5.2.

Ellis then arranged the material for jazz band; some of his musicians even took solos in these complex additive meters.

ACTIVITY 6.4 *Listening to and singing along with CD track 29*
Listen to the recording of Don Ellis's "Bulgarian Bulge" on CD track 29 as you follow the transcription of the "head" in figure 5.2. Try clapping along with the recording. Try singing the tune on the syllables "da, da, da" and clapping along.

Outside the circle of professional musicians who borrowed Bulgarian music for their own compositions, groups of people who called themselves "international folk dancers" based an important aspect of their social life on Bulgarian music and dance culture. Located in community centers and on college campuses in the 1960s, and continuing in a somewhat attenuated form today, members of folk dance clubs danced mainly traditional line dances from the Balkans and Israel plus a few couple dances from Norway and Sweden (figure 6.1). Bulgarian dances were especially prized for their fast tempos, additive meters, and relatively complicated sets of choreographed variations on basic steps. The dances were both intellectually engaging and physically challenging. American and Canadian dance teachers learned the dances from professional ensembles and village groups in Bulgaria and other parts of the Balkans and returned home to teach them. They also collected and reissued recordings for the dancers to use. Eventually some American musicians learned the music well enough to play it for dancers. American international folk dancers used Bulgarian music and dance to create their own intimate social world within the larger American society and their own aesthetic pleasure without really understanding very much about Bulgarian culture and the sources of these dances and dance music (Lausevic 1998).

ACTIVITY 6.5 *Dancing to CD track 30*
Listen to CD track 30, recorded by a group of American women who learned to play Bulgarian traditional instruments (figure 6.2).

Begin by finding the beat of their kopanitsa, *the generic name for Bulgarian dances in a meter of 11. The notation of the first two melodies in figure 6.3 may help. The meter is organized into beats of two and three pulses that total eleven pulses: 2 + 2 + 3 + 2 + 2 = 11. This meter can be expressed in different ways:*

short	short	long	short	short
clap	clap	clap	clap	clap
1	2	3	4	5
1-2	1-2	1-2-3	1-2	1-2
1-2	3-4	5-6-7	8-9	10-11

Once you can clap along with the rhythm, you can dance to it. Each step indicated below occurs on one of the five main beats you were clapping.

The dance pattern is three measures of eleven pulses (or of five main beats). Begin by forming an open circle holding hands with your body facing to the center and your weight on your left foot.

Measure 1, beat 1: Step to the right onto your right foot.

Measure 1, beat 2: Step onto your left foot behind the right foot.

Measure 1, beat 3: Step to the right onto your right foot.

Measure 1, beat 4: Hop on your right foot in place.

Measure 1, beat 5: Step onto your left foot in front of your right foot.

Measure 2, beat 1: Step to the right onto your right foot.

Measure 2, beat 2: Step onto your left foot behind the right foot.

Measure 2, beat 3: Step to the right onto your right foot.

Measure 2, beat 4: Step onto your left foot in front of your right foot.

Measure 2, beat 5: Step onto your right foot in place (slightly behind your left foot).

Measure 3, beat 1: Step to the left onto your left foot.

Measure 3, beat 2: Step onto your right foot behind the left foot.

Measure 3, beat 3: Step to the left onto your left foot.

Measure 3, beat 4: Step onto your right foot in front of your left foot.

Measure 3, beat 5: Step onto your left foot in place (slightly behind your right foot).

Repeat this pattern to the end of the dance.

Because the dance pattern is in three measures and the music is in four measures, the beginning of the dance step and the musical phrase correspond only every twelve measures, adding to the pleasure of the dance-and-music experience.

FIGURE 6.1 *American international folk dancers.* *(Photo by Flora Grolimund Cannavj courtesy of* Folk Dance Scene *magazine, 2000)*

FIGURE 6.2 Medna Usta (*figuratively, "Sweet Voice"*), an American group playing Bulgarian music. From left to right, Barb Cordes (tarambuka), Karen Guggenheim-Machlis (gaida), Anne Cleveland (tambura), Dena Bjornlie (gŭdulka), Ruth Hunter (accordion), 1988. (Photo courtesy of Karen Guggenheim-Machlis)

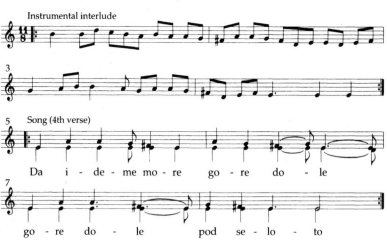

FIGURE 6.3 The kopanitsa on CD track 30.

This is a relatively simple dance, but it is still quite fun to do. It is an introduction to some of the more complicated and physically demanding dances that international folk dancers continue to enjoy. One of the pleasures of this kind of dancing is the sense of community created by a circle of people all doing the same steps at the same time. This coordinated movement of a community, symbolically closed in on itself, is an important part of the attraction of these dances for American folk dancers—and for Bulgarians as well.

Recording technology was a critical element in the popularity of "world music" traditions in the 1960s. Among the LP records of Bulgarian folk music released in the United States in the 1960s, the recording of the Koutev choir on the Nonesuch label had an enormous impact. It spawned a tradition of unaccompanied women's singing groups that imitate these recordings (CD track 31). Many young American women first heard this music in the heady days of the women's liberation movement of the 1960s. They heard in this women's music from Bulgaria a new way of being female with a powerful, loud, direct, all-female sound unlike anything available to them in American culture. They seemed to embrace the sound as a symbol and expression of an alternative way of being and feeling female. In choosing to learn to perform in this style, it became more than a symbol. It was a form of social behavior in an all-female organization. Their understandings and performances gave the ostensibly foreign and slightly exotic music of Bulgaria new meaning and life in an American context. The attraction these choirs hold for non-Bulgarian women has continued, and in the year 2002 many of them can be found in the United States, Western Europe, and Japan.

ACTIVITY 6.6 *Listening to CD track 31*
Listen to CD track 31, a recording of American women singing a Bulgarian song arranged for an unaccompanied choir. Compare their sound to the sound of the Bulgarian choirs on CD tracks 21, 23, and 25. How did they do?

Over the last one hundred years or so, Americans and Europeans have assigned all kinds of significance to music from other cultures, including to Bulgarian music. These include hearing it as an art, giving it

new symbolic meanings, organizing social groups around its performance, and treating it as a commodity by buying recordings of it or
adding it to their own products. Though the meanings they assign are
often different from and irrelevant to the original meanings its Bulgarian makers give to it, American interest and the commercial implications of that interest have contributed to Bulgarians' pride in their own
traditions. In the postcommunist period, when support for folk arts has
dwindled, a number of well-known Bulgarian professional musicians,
singers, and dancers have immigrated to the United States in an effort
to capitalize on Americans' interest in their culture.

CHAPTER 7

A New Music for a New Era

In the summer of 2000 I returned to Bulgaria to learn what had become of traditional music in the eleven years since the fall of the communist regime in November 1989. Some changes were predictable. I assumed, for example, that state support for the arts, and in particular the folk arts, might have declined because the ideological underpinnings of such support had been swept away. That prediction turned out to be true.

Many of the professional folk ensembles in provincial towns had shut down for lack of support. Some continued on a private basis but reduced the number of performers to make themselves economically viable. Only the most central ensembles such as the Koutev ensemble and the folk orchestra of Radio and Television Sofia persevered in something like their old form, supported by government ministries. Some choirs and ensembles existed only for occasional performances but no longer provided their members with a regular salary as they had during the communist period. They rehearsed mainly to prepare for tours abroad to feed the interest in the mystery of the Bulgarian voices. Even where ensembles provided a salary for musicians, those salaries were now so meager that many musicians quit the ensembles to pursue jobs unrelated to music in the new private economy. Some even left the country to seek their fortunes in western Europe and the United States, preferring a brighter future for their children to their lives as professional musicians.

Wedding music was also on the wane. With the demise of communism, it had lost its political meaning as a form of antigovernment expression. The economics of weddings had changed as well. The transition to a market economy has been long and difficult for Bulgarians, and many feel themselves to be worse off economically now than they were during the communist regime. Although many more consumer goods are available than in the past, including those from fashionable retailers like Levi Strauss, Gucci, and Christian Dior, the prices are out of reach of average Bulgarians. Instead of saving up for symbolic display on music at weddings, ordinary people have little money to spend at all. As a consequence, the market for wedding music has dried up, and people are employing disc jockeys or having weddings without music. Like their counterparts in the state-supported folk music ensembles, some very well known wedding musicians have left Bulgaria, dreaming of a better life abroad.

I also predicted that there might be renewed interest in the informal performance of unarranged forms of village music and old rituals that had been banned as religious or superstitious by the communist government. To assess this possibility, I attended the national folk festival for amateur singers, dancers, and instrumentalists, held every five years in the beautiful town of Koprivshtitsa in the mountains about sixty miles east of Sofia. Koprivshtitsa has been preserved as a museum of nineteenth-century Ottoman-period house architecture (figure 7.1). This festival and similar local and regional festivals had been an important means of supporting approved forms of traditional music, song, and dance during the communist period. Though attenuated, the support for this sort of activity continues, and the 2000 festival was the third in the postcommunist period. The festival provided some evidence of a resurgence of interest in folk music at the village level.

FIGURE 7.1 *Koprivshtitsa house architecture.* *(Timothy Rice, 2000)*

Surprisingly, a number of singing groups from the Shop region included young girls. When I researched this kind of singing in the 1970s, I recorded only older singers, typically in their fifties and sixties (Rice 1977). They complained then that girls were no longer interested in this style of singing, and even if they were interested, they were so used to hearing modern forms of music that they could no longer "squash" the intervals properly to achieve the correct "ringing" effect. For Koprivshtitsa in 2000 many villages sent two groups of singers—one of older women and one of young girls. The girls sang very well, with a good feeling for the traditional harmonic intervals and ornaments required by the style. It seems that there may be a resurgence of interest in traditional, unarranged forms of music among youngsters living in villages—and even among some young urbanites. Perhaps because the music has been freed of its political connections to the communist regime, it has once again become a pleasant form of social behavior and an art form for young people in the villages—and that bodes well for the future of the tradition (figure 7.2).

FIGURE 7.2 *A singing group at the Koprivshtitsa festival.* *(Timothy Rice, 2000)*

A NEW FUSION OF FOLK AND POPULAR MUSIC

The fate of the three most important streams of traditional music practice in the communist period—professional, arranged folklore; amateur village ensembles; and wedding music—was partly predictable given the political and economic changes after 1989. I was completely surprised—though perhaps I shouldn't have been—by the rise of a new kind of music that had not existed before.

Generally ethnomusicologists believe that music is linked to cultural, social, political, and economic systems and therefore that music changes as culture, society, politics, and economics change. However, we don't have very sure ways of predicting precisely how music will change. In the wake of such changes, new meanings may be assigned to old musical forms, or one form may decline in importance while another one increases in importance. In the case of radical social or cultural change, none of the old forms may be adequate, and new forms of music may be required. In the summer of 2000 Bulgarians were variously enthralled and repelled by a new form of music that seemed to be serving the new needs of a society in transition from communism to capitalism and from totalitarianism to democracy (Rice 2002).

That new form of music is a mix of Euro-American popular music with Rom, Serbian, Turkish, Greek, Romanian, and Macedonian styles, with only an occasional nod to Bulgarian traditional music. The new style had new names: *popfolk* and *chalga*. *Popfolk* is formed from the English words "popular" and "folk." This label captures the symbolic link of the genre to a new, westernized form of modernity and is meant to distance the genre from any association with the labels used in the communist period, when what is understood in English as folk music was called *narodna muzika* ("people's music") and what is understood as popular music was called *estradna* ("stage") *muzika*. *Chalga*, on the other hand, is formed from a Turkish word meaning "musical instrument." Rom instrumentalists are commonly called *chalgadzhii* ("instrumentalists"), and the word captures the association of the genre with Roma and Rom music and with Turkish cultural influence, a negative link for many Bulgarians.

This new Bulgarian music has become extremely popular. A Bulgarian scholar told me that sales of recordings in this style currently account for more than 80 percent of the music market for cassettes and compact discs. Two private radio stations and a cable television station broadcast this kind of music. I interviewed programmers for the two radio stations and some of the artists involved in the scene and spent a fair bit of time in Sofia listening to the radio, watching television, and visiting dance clubs in an effort to understand the scope and nature of this new genre: Bulgarian *popfolk* music.

THE ROOTS OF *POPFOLK*

New genres of music rarely, if ever, spring fully formed from the head of a brilliant composer or musician. Rather, each new musical genre has its roots in existing music, which is manipulated, reworked, and renamed to meet new artistic, cultural, social, political, and economic demands. The development of *popfolk* certainly worked that way.

Popfolk is an outgrowth of Bulgarian Rom music and the music of Bulgaria's Balkan neighbors. Not coincidentally, these kinds of music were not supported during the last ten years of the communist period. As we saw in chapter 5, the government banned Rom music as aggressive antistate display, but it had been enormously popular at least partly for that reason as well. The music of Bulgaria's Balkan neighbors had also been popular during the communist period as a reaction against the nationalist and communist ideology of the state and against the folk music promoted by the state as representative of that ideology. So during the communist period many people had tuned out the national radio station that broadcast that music and that ideology and tuned in to Serbian, Greek, and Turkish radio stations, which broadcast new forms of popular music that Bulgarians could relate to—music with a Balkan accent. For most of the 1980s those dissatisfied with the communist government and the music it supported favored Rom, Serbian, Greek, and Turkish music, as well as rock music, even though they couldn't hear it on the national Bulgarian stations and were forbidden from playing it themselves.

After 1989 there were no government impediments to experiments with new musical styles. Bulgarian musicians began to write their own lyrics in Bulgarian to well-known melodies from Rom, Macedonian, Serbian, Turkish, and Greek hit songs. In this way, they made what were foreign musical styles into a Bulgarian style, an example of a cultural process called "appropriation" or more simply, "borrowing."

The basic musical marker of *popfolk* is the Rom *kyuchek* rhythm—or more precisely, *kyuchek* rhythms. As a form of Rom music, *kyucheks* either are played as instrumentals or have words in Romany. As such, they are markers of difference but also symbols of a kind of freedom of expression denied to Bulgarians during the communist period. One of the two basic *kyuchek* rhythms is a duple meter (the other is in 9 = 2 + 2 + 2 + 3), which can have a couple of rhythmic realizations (CD track 32). The most basic duple rhythmic pattern, and the main one appropriated for *popfolk*, has a distinctive, repeated bass and drum pattern, in other words, a rhythmic ostinato. The pattern can be graphically represented in the following way:

Beats:	1	2
Implicit pulses:	1234	1234
Bass/drum beat:	x . .x	x. x.
Musical Notation	♩. ♪♩♩	

> **ACTIVITY 7.1** *Listening to CD track 32*
> *Listen to CD track 32, an instrumental* kyuchek *featuring a clarinet soloist. Follow the beat outlined in the text. Many aspects of the style are interpreted as Rom and "oriental," including the use of microtones, certain ornaments, and slides from pitch to pitch.*

Serbians had already appropriated that beat in the 1970s to create a new genre of Serbian popular music called "newly composed folk music." Bulgarians heard this genre on the radio during the 1980s and borrowed from it to create their own songs after 1989, when they had the freedom to do so. The *popfolk* song on CD track 33 has many notable musical elements besides this distinctive rhythm. First, the introduction begins with the synthesized sound of the *gaida* playing first the characteristic descending fifth that opens many performances on the instrument and then the instrumental interlude between the song verses. The *gaida* sound and the text signal the Bulgarian character of the song. Second, the use of a vase-shaped hand drum called *tarambuka* and the E scale or Phrygian scale (EFGABCDE) are characteristics associated with Rom music in Bulgaria. Third, the sounds created by a synthesizer, electric bass, and drum kit are modern, linking the song to modernity in other parts of Europe and the world. Through a combination of these musical elements, this song symbolizes and articulates its place and the place of its makers and fans within Bulgarian, Rom, and modern cultures.

ACTIVITY 7.2 *Listening to CD track 33*
Listen to CD track 33, a popfolk song in the Bulgarian language using the kyuchek *rhythm. Notice the underlying* kyuchek *rhythmic pattern in the bass and drums; the sound of the synthesized* gaida; *the Phrygian scale; and the modern electronically produced sound. The lyrics and the title, a Bulgarian expression ("Every wonder in three days") that suggests that all things good and bad disappear in three days, advise those who worry too much not to poison themselves with worries, a sentiment especially relevant in tough times.*

Though *kyucheks* provide the most common rhythm in *popfolk* music, it is by no means the only one. Slow balladlike pop songs are also popular, as well as rhythms associated with swing jazz, Latin music, Greek urban music (*rebetika*), and occasionally a Bulgarian traditional song (CD track 34). When Bulgarian traditional songs are performed in the *popfolk* style, a modern band featuring synthesizers accompanies them, and the rhythms and lyrics are sometimes changed to give the songs a modern twist.

ACTIVITY 7.3 *Listening to CD track 34*
Listen to CD track 34, a traditional song entitled "Kara Kolyo sideshe" (Black Kolyo sat). Performed by a young popfolk singer named Extra Nina, she executes traditional ornamentation, including glottal stops, with great skill. The song lyrics deal with a traditional theme, the tension created when old, ugly, or drunken men go after attractive young women.

THE LYRICS OF *POPFOLK* MUSIC

With the exception of a few traditional songs, *popfolk* lyrics focus mainly on contemporary themes in a contemporary language using rhyme. These features of *popfolk* song texts contrast with the lyrics of traditional Bulgarian songs. Traditional songs don't use rhyme, and they deal with many features of life, such as calendar rituals and patterns of work, that have largely disappeared. Even love, courtship, and marriage, one of the most important themes of both traditional and *popfolk* lyrics, were experienced in a very different way before World War II than after it. Indeed, the irrelevance of many folk song texts to modern life contributes to the decline of this tradition.

Popfolk songwriters have responded to that relevance gap by inventing new texts on modern themes, including current events such as devaluation of the currency, the increasing crime rate, poverty that keeps young people from marrying, and such seemingly mundane topics as vacationing at the Black Sea and taking the train to Istanbul (CD track 35). Instead of climbing on a horse or a cart as they do in folk songs, *popfolk* singers dream of owning BMWs. For many Bulgarians, one of the most shocking new themes in *popfolk* is sex, treated graphically though always with humor. One song popular in 2000, "Monika, Monika, Monika," even makes fun in astonishing detail of the Monica Lewinsky–Bill Clinton scandal of the late 1990s. By employing modern forms of speech and treating contemporary themes, these songs are more meaningful than traditional folk song texts for today's listeners, especially young people.

ACTIVITY 7.4 *Listening to CD track 35*
Listen to CD track 35, a popfolk song called "Zet zavryan." Zet means "son-in-law," and a zavryan zet is a son-in-law who lives after marriage in the home of his wife's parents. This is contrary to tradition, which mandates that the couple should live at the groom's parents' home or alone in a home provided for them by his parents. Being a zavryan zet is therefore considered shameful but is a fact of modern economic life. In this humorous song, the singer complains that, in spite of being a sweet and dutiful son-in-law, he can never satisfy his mother-in-law, who hangs over him like an ax ready to fall.

PERFORMANCES OF *POPFOLK* SONGS

The performance style of *popfolk* is as thoroughly modern as the lyrics and the instruments. The biggest stars of *popfolk* are young women, who dress provocatively and move their hips and bodies sexily in motions

related to social dancing in America, Rom *kyucheks*, and Middle Eastern belly dance styles. Influenced perhaps by Madonna, the singers typically use one name, often a modern one such as Gloria, Kamelia, and
Lia. The female singers are routinely referred to in newspapers as
"sexbombs," a label justified by their mock-sexual moves and poses,
combined with their revealing dresses, heavy makeup, and sultry looks
(figure 7.3). This look is most surprising, at least to me, when the singers
sing traditional songs with traditional vocal timbre and expertly ren-
dered vocal ornamentation, as on CD track 34.

I interviewed a *popfolk* singer named Tsvetelina, and it turned out
that her background included deep roots in folk music (CD track 36).
After hearing that I first became interested in Bulgarian music through
dancing, she said:

> Interestingly, I was also a dancer. I danced folk dances for all of eight
> years before a love of folk music was born in me. My parents were
> performers of Macedonian folk songs. My father was an accordionist

FIGURE 7.3 Popfolk *singer Tsvetelina, from an album cover.* *(Courtesy of Payner
Studio)*

and in general I was nursed on folk songs. My mother said that when I was only a month old, I was backstage at one of their concerts. From first grade, that means I was seven years old, I danced folk dances and began to sing in a children's ensemble that even won a gold medal, of which I'm very proud. In fact, dancing was more interesting for me than singing.

I am now twenty-four years old, and although I am acquainted with traditional folklore, in general I was raised on more contemporary folklore, from the time when all folk musicians began to make more modern arrangements. But besides those arrangements, a lot of Serbian, Greek, and Turkish music was listened to. After all, we are in the Balkans. At home my parents loved to listen to Shaban Shaulich and Vesna Zmianats [Serbian singers]. She was my favorite. I learned a lot from her. The [radio and cassette] market was full of Serbian and Greek songs. Then, after I finished school, I began to sing. Serbian music was mainly heard. There was no Bulgarian music [of this type on the radio]. Now mainly Bulgarian music is heard [on the radio]. In those days folk ensembles began to do exactly *popfolk* songs, even ballads that were not characteristic of folk music, but they did these "folk ballads" in the rhythm of Macedonian songs. People began to want to hear these songs in Bulgarian. For that reason they translated these Serbian, Greek, and Turkish songs into Bulgarian.

Tsvetelina's comments indicate both her roots in and love of Bulgarian traditional music and her thoroughly modern musical tastes. She enjoyed singing folk songs from Macedonia, Thrace, and Strandzha and put a few of them on each of her albums. Tellingly, she said that she would perform more of them if she thought there was a market for them, but she did not believe that there was, and so she sang mainly *popfolk* songs.

ACTIVITY 7.5 *Listening and dancing to CD track 36*
Listen to the popfolk *song by Tsvetelina on CD track 36. The singer tells her lover that, although she is satisfied with their relationship, she feels like a bird in a cage, unable to sing. The melody is just the kind of folk ballad she describes in the text. The song melody contains no references to Bulgarian folk styles, but the instrumental interlude between the verses and the underlying beat are typical of Macedonian traditional dance music. Try dancing* pravo horo *to it.*

Though *popfolk* sells more recordings than any other kind of music in Bulgaria today, *popfolk* singers and musicians make most of their money by performing at concerts and in dance clubs and restaurants. To check out the scene, I went one night to probably the most famous dance club devoted to this music, Fajtona ("The Phaeton"). The music at the club, on the ground floor of a drab, gray building near the edge of the center of Sofia, started around midnight and continued until morning. As a few friends and I passed through the door around 12:30 A.M., three men checked our bags looking for weapons. It turns out that *popfolk* music, as well as the clubs and discos devoted to it, is a favorite of Bulgarian gangsters, who have flourished in the postcommunist period. A long hall painted with frescoes of Sofia streets at the turn of the last century, scenes including elegant, horse-drawn carriages (phaetons), led to a restaurant with tables and booths laid out around a dance floor. It wasn't crowded yet, but seven or eight tables of customers were scattered around the room. A band of four Rom musicians was playing loudly. Two synthesizers, clarinet, and drum set put out a wonderfully rich, thick sound. A man and two women danced solo using the generic pop dance moves of this new style. Occasionally two women in belly dance costumes joined them on the floor to dance casually. As the night wore on, the drummer was invited from time to time to one of the tables to play in exchange for a tip. He carried to the table a set of two small drums on a stand, similar to the timbales of salsa music. Often one person danced solo by the table to the delight of his or her friends. The belly dancers also began to circulate around the room, searching for tips by dancing provocatively next to male customers, including, to my embarrassment and the amusement of my companions, me. The club was a place where Roma and Bulgarians could dance, enjoy Rom-based popular music together, and relax after (or before) a day's work.

In Sofia, one cable video channel was devoted entirely to *popfolk*. Some videos documented concert performances and others contained stagings of the content of the lyrics. The concerts typically presented a potpourri of singers, often affiliated with a particular record company. The female singers looked beautiful and moved suggestively. The audiences contained a huge age range, from young children between six and twelve years of age to teenagers and young adults to the forty-something parents of the children. It seems that *popfolk* appeals to people of nearly every generation. Young boys and girls were allowed onstage to give flowers and sometimes exchange a hug or kiss on the cheek with the performers. This behavior, it seemed to me, diffused the sexuality of the performances and reminded me of the teenybopper response to the sexuality of Madonna's material girl and Britney Spears.

Videos that act out the text of a song vary in mood depending on the lyrics. Since the lyrics so often deal with love, the videos often show people experiencing problems in their relationships—or they treat such problems jokingly. The video illustrating the folk song "Kara Kolyo sideshe" (CD track 34), for example, concerns an old man counting his money, spending it freely in a tavern, and behaving lecherously toward a pair of young women while being unfaithful to a third. The video cuts back and forth between traditional scenes and modern ones, suggesting that such male behavior is a constant. In the end, the women outsmart the man, a traditional theme of folk songs, most of which were made up by and sung by women (Rice 1994: 115–26).

POPFOLK AS ART, SYMBOL, COMMODITY, AND BEHAVIOR

Popfolk began as an artistic phenomenon with political implications. That is, it is an appropriation of what once was considered, during the communist regime, foreign and decadent and therefore tightly controlled. The musical styles on which it is based were popular at least in part because of their status as forbidden fruit under the previous totalitarian regime. Their adoption as a favorite expressive form was partly a political act in a new era of relative freedom. The political aspect of *popfolk* has continued to be controversial throughout its brief history.

Popfolk is problematic for many Bulgarians because it flies in the face of everything the communist government stood for. Although the most heinous elements of the totalitarianism of that government are gone and not lamented, many of its values live on, including values expressed in music and other arts. *Popfolk* challenges those values and thus provokes controversy for at least four reasons among those who retain some of the old views.

The first problem is that *popfolk* is based less on ostensibly Bulgarian musical traditions than it is on foreign or minority ones. For many people raised under a government that constructed and promoted Bulgarian nationalism in music, the popularity of *popfolk* with masses of people, and the relative absence of Bulgarian folk music styles on the airwaves, is an affront to their national feelings. That the songs are in

Bulgarian is not enough to satisfy them. They hear in the music references to Rom, Turkish, Serbian, and Greek styles, and they are not pleased. Many who hold this view profess to hate the music and not to listen to it. This is a good example of the way aesthetic preferences often develop from political views.

A related problem, the fact that Rom musical styles, instrumentalists, and singers are at the center of much of *popfolk* music, is galling to many Bulgarians. While many critics take what seems to be an aesthetic stand against the music, at least one Bulgarian writer has pointed out that racism and negative attitudes toward Roma may be at the center of some people's distaste for this music (Levi 2000).

When people condemn *popfolk* as cheap and tasteless music, they are referring primarily to the sex-filled song texts but also to the use of Rom musical styles and the ethnicity and appearance of the singers. Whatever is lowbrow about *popfolk*, however, is a completely conscious reaction by its makers to the highbrow tone of communist culture and propaganda. Classical music values provided the methods for arranging traditional music during the communist period, when the communists scorned everything in every domain that was deemed "cheap" or "tasteless" or "dirty." *Popfolk* thus is a way of letting off steam for some Bulgarians—steam that scalds other Bulgarians.

Second, one of the big issues surrounding *popfolk* is whether it is essentially a commercial, commodified genre or whether it has artistic value. Those who don't like it condemn it as essentially a commercial form. Those who make it claim to create their music in an artistic way and point to the prize-winning poets who now compose some of the song texts and to the university-level music educations of some of the musicians. Art and taste can clearly coexist with commodification, but many who do not like a particular kind of music use its commercial popularity as a stick to beat it with.

Third, many educated Bulgarians are worried about their position in the world. Bulgaria has just left behind four decades in the "eastern bloc" and, not too many years before that, more than four hundred years in the Ottoman Empire. They feel, in other words, that for most of their history they have been cut off from the main developments in European culture. This history of isolation strikes at their self-confidence, as it puts their status as "Europeans" in question. University students, intellectuals, business leaders, and politicians hope that Bulgaria will soon become a full-fledged member of what they call "the European family." For such people, *popfolk* is an affront because its use of Balkan forms of music harkens back to a benighted past that they would prefer to put behind them and forget. For such people, *popfolk* glamorizes Bulgaria's position in a marginalized part of Europe that has never been fully part of the European mainstream. Many of my friends who rather liked *popfolk* music took pride in their Balkan heritage and felt no shame and indeed a certain pride in considering themselves as thoroughly Balkan people. Those who seek Bulgaria's future in a modern Europe, however, tend to prefer popular styles of music, such as rock and rap, associated with western Europe and the United States—another example of politics preceding aesthetics.

Fourth, while much of the politics of *popfolk* is implicit, it also includes some explicit political commentary that is all the more effective because of the style's far-reaching popularity. Though most singers focus mostly on the mundane aspects of modern life, a few use the songs to make more serious points about the political life of the country. One of the most notorious groups in this regard is Ku-ku Bend, which performs with a theatrical company called Hŭshove ("Revolutionaries"), a reference to the late nineteenth-century figures who founded the Bulgarian state. The group consists of young Bulgarians in their twenties and thirties. Outstanding musicians with university educations in classical music, they have mastered the Rom and other ethnic styles of *popfolk* music. They use their skill in a self-conscious way for political and social commentary so pointed that the national television station canceled their show. It has since reappeared as a popular show on an otherwise little-watched cable station. One two-part suite of theirs is called "Do Chikago" ("To Chicago") and "I nazad" ("And back"). The titles are taken from a famous nineteenth-century Bulgarian travelogue called *Do Chikago i nazad* that described its author's trip to America, a book that many Bulgarians have read with keen interest. "Do Chikago" is a parody of a tango song, "Por una cabeza" (For a cow), composed in 1935 by Carlos Cardel, an Argentinian, and heard by Bulgarians in the 1992 American film *Scent of a Woman*. The lyrics ask, metaphorically, what will happen to me, to my sense of self, if I go to the West or if I go sniffing after the sort of seductive Western values represented by the tango (CD track 37). "I nazad" transforms the tango melody into an instrumental Rom *kyuchek* in a nine-beat $(2 + 2 + 2 + 3)$ meter, answering the question posed by the lyrics in "Do Chikago" in musically symbolic terms (CD track 38). The answer, it seems to me, is that Bulgarians' inescapable essence is Balkan, not western European or American.

ACTIVITY 7.6 *Listening to CD tracks 37 and 38*
*Listen to CD tracks 37 and 38. Notice that the second piece
uses the same melody as the first but transforms its rhythm from
a duple meter with a tango feel into a* kyuchek *in 9 = 2 +
2 + 2 + 3. The orchestration for brass band evokes a popular
style of southern Serbian Rom music.*

Popfolk participates simultaneously in many cultural and social domains. It is an art form that is produced extraordinarily well by its makers and loved by many fans. At the same time, its value as a commodity influences aspects of its form and some artistic choices. It also has
symbolic cultural implications, since it is interpreted as telling political
stories about Bulgarians' position in the modern world and their sense
of history. Its performances also model new, perhaps future, forms of
social behavior, such as the public display of female sexuality and the
potential cultural centrality of the socially marginalized Roma.

MUSICAL CHANGE AND MUSICAL SIGNIFICANCE

The way *popfolk* music operates in Bulgaria today is similar to the way
other forms of Bulgarian music have functioned in the past. I end this
overview of Bulgarian music by stating two general principles that
probably apply to music the world over.

First, music is never static. It changes as culture and society change.
Athough some people may regard certain older forms of music as "authentic" and perhaps in that sense timeless, the stories about Bulgarian
music in this book illustrate the principle that every type of music has
a history. Traditional genres may be older than some genres of modern
music, but every surviving example of traditional music itself super-
seded even older ways of making music. If authenticity is to retain any
meaning at all, it has to mean that music is authentic when it responds
in some meaningful way to the culture and society around it, as it virtually always does.

A second important principle is that aesthetic values and taste in music are not autonomous domains of culture or thought or feeling. A person's or a people's aesthetic preferences are part and parcel of the cultural, social, political, and economic life in which music is performed

(Rice 2003). As culture, music is often interpreted as having symbolic meanings, including political ones. As social behavior, music is one expression of social relations—real ones such as the different opportunities afforded men and women or hoped-for ones such as equality for women and fair treatment of minorities. As a part of economic life, music can provide a means of income, and its patronage by private clients, the state, or the general public can have a powerful effect on the quality of music and the personal and aesthetic choices that musicians make. The significance of music knows few bounds. It is certainly not merely an art form or a type of entertainment, though it can be those things as well. For it to be appreciated, supported, patronized, and subjected to limitless hours of devoted practice, music must fulfill many roles in human life.

Glossary of Bulgarian Terms

Bairaktarki: Female flag bearers.

Bavna pesen, bavni pesni: "Slow song(s)"; a nonmetrical song melody.

Buchi: "Bellows"; description of an accompanying voice in a polyphonic song.

Chalga: Turkish for "musical instrument"; a genre of *popfolk* music popular in the 1990s.

Chalgadzhii: Instrumentalists, especially Rom instrumentalists.

Daichovo horo: An open-circle dance in a meter of $9 = 2 + 2 + 2 + 3$.

Estradna muzika: "Stage music"; popular music during the communist period.

Gaida: Bagpipe made from a goatskin with a blowpipe, melody pipe, and drone pipe.

Gaidanitsa: The melody pipe of the *gaida*.

Gaidar: Bagpiper.

Gŭdulka: Pear-shaped bowed lute with three playing strings and eight or so sympathetic strings.

Haiduti: Guerilla fighters against the Turks during the Ottoman period.

Horo: An open-circle or line dance formed by dancers holding hands.

Izvikva: "Cries out"; description of the leading voice in a polyphonic song.

Kaba gaida: "Big bagpipe," characteristic of the Rhodope Mountain region.

Kaval: End-blown, rim-blown, bevel-edged wooden flute with seven fingerholes, a thumbhole, and three "devil's holes" for tuning.

Koledari: Christmas carolers.

Koledarski pesni: Songs for *koleda*, a Christmas-caroling ritual.

Kopanitsa: Open-circle dance in $11 = 2 + 2 + 3 + 2 + 2$

Krivo plovdivsko horo: "Crooked dance from the Plovdiv region"; a dance in $13 = 2 + 2 + 2 + 3 + 2 + 2$.

Kukerovden: *Kukers'* ("masqueraders") day, the carnival before Lent.

Kukersko horo: The dance of the *kukers* ("masqueraders").

Kum: The godfather of a married couple's children.

Kyuchek: Rom solo dance with rapid hip movements.

Makedonsko horo: "Macedonian dance"; an open-circle dance in a meter of $7 = 3 + 2 + 2$.

Muzika: "Music," but specifically instrumental, and especially classical, instrumental music.

Muzikant, muzikanti: Musician, musicians, especially professional musicians.

Narodna muzika: "People's music"; folk music; music supported by the communist government.

Peene: Singing.

Pesen: Song.

Popfolk: Pan-Balkan, Bulgarian-language song style popular in the 1990s.

Pravo horo: "Straight dance," the most basic Bulgarian open-circle dance in a duple meter.

Rŭchenitsa: Solo dance in a meter of $7 = 2 + 2 + 3$, especially important at weddings.

Rŭka: Hand.

Sedenkarski pesni: "Sitting songs"; songs sung at *sedyanki*.

Sedyanka, sedyanki: "Sitting, sittings"; autumnal communal occasions for work, singing songs, and courting.

Shalvari: Traditional pants worn by Muslim women.

Shop: An adjective naming a subgroup of Bulgarians who live around Sofia.

Slaga: "Follows"; description of an accompanying voice in a polyphonic song.

Smeseno horo: "Mixed dance"; an instrumental tune that combines various additive meters.

Sŭbori: Village fairs, an important occasion for music, song, and dance.

Sŭvet: Council, the governing body of a political jurisdiction during the communist period.

Tambura: Long-necked, fretted lute plucked with a plectrum.

Tarambuka: Single-headed, vase-shaped drum played with the hands.

Tŭpan: Cylindrical, double-headed bass drum played with a large stick on one head and a thin wand on the other.

Velikden: "Great Day"; Easter.

Zet: Son-in-law.

Zhŭtvarski pesni: Harvest songs.

Glossary of Musical Terms

A cappella: Singing choral music without instrumental accompaniment.

Additive meter: The grouping of regular pulses in units of 2 and 3, which are then added together to form meters of 5, 7, 9, 11, and so forth.

Antiphony, antiphonal singing: A performance practice involving two groups of equal or similar size singing the same music in alternation.

Arpeggio, arpeggiation, arpeggiated: A chord whose pitches are sounded successively to form a melody.

Beat: A regularly recurring time pattern in music that often generates hand clapping or foot tapping as a response.

Chord, block chord: A set of simultaneously sounding pitches.

Chromaticism, chromatic: The use of all twelve pitches contained in an octave.

Consonance, consonant: Intervals or chords that sound relatively relaxed, stable, or pleasant.

Countermelody: A secondary melody accompanying the main melody.

Counterpoint: The combination of two or more melodic lines.

Degree of a scale: An ordinal count of the notes in a scale from the tonal center up, that is, first degree, second degree, and so forth.

Dissonance, dissonant: Intervals or chords that sound relatively tense, unstable, or discordant.

Drone: A single pitch (or a set of pitches) sounded continuously, as on the bagpipe, or intermittently, as when singers break up the pitch to pronounce words.

Duple meter: A grouping of musical time into two regular, repeated beats, counted 121212.

Eighth note: A note value that normally represents half a beat.

Falsetto: In singing, the highest register of the voice, produced with head resonance rather than chest resonance.

Glottal stop: In singing, the momentary closing of the glottis to produce a kind of hitting sound.

Grace note: In musical notation, a small note of short duration written next to the main melody note.

Half note: A note value that normally represents two beats.

Harmony: A set of simultaneously sounding pitches, also called a chord; the system of relationships among chords in a particular musical style.

Homophony, homophonic style: "Same voice"; song texture in which all the parts move in the same or similar rhythm; a texture employing melody accompanied by chords.

Interval: The distance between two pitches.

Key: In tonal music, the pitch relationships that establish one pitch as the tonic or central pitch and the others as subordinate; in Western music there are twenty-four keys, twelve of them major and twelve minor, forming the "tonal system."

Key change: Moving among the twenty-four keys in the Western tonal system.

Lute: Any stringed instrument with a resonating body and a neck.

Melody: A series of pitches in succession that is the main focus of musical attention in a song or instrumental piece; a tune.

Meter: The organization of pulsation.

Motive: A melodic or rhythmic fragment used to construct a larger musical entity, such as a phrase or complete melody.

Nonmetrical: An approach to rhythm with no regular beat or pulsation.

Octave: The melodic or harmonic interval spanning eight scale degrees; both pitches are given the same name, and the frequency of the higher note is twice that of the lower.

Ornaments, ornamentation: Tones of short duration added to the main melodic tones; defines the style of performance and can be an indicator of the skill of the performer.

Ostinato: Constantly recurring melodic, rhythmic, or harmonic motive.

Phrase: A melodic unit or musical thought that forms part of a complete musical idea such as a song verse.

Phrygian scale: The E scale (EFGABCDE), popular in Rom music and *popfolk.*

Pitch: The quality of "highness" or "lowness" of tones, measured as the frequency of vibration (the number cycles per second) of the sound wave.

Polyphony, polyphonic singing: "Many sounds"; musical texture of two or more melodic parts performed together.

Quarter note: A note value that normally represents one beat.

Range: The distance, often measured in scale degrees, from the highest to the lowest pitch in a melody, scale, song, or instrumental part.

Refrain: Repeating text in a song, added to a verse.

Rhythm: The organization of durations in a piece of music; in general, the time dimension in music.

Scale: A set of pitches used in a piece or style of music and presented in ascending order.

Suite: A set of short songs or instrumental dances performed in succession without pause to create a long, varied piece.

Texture: The relationships among the parts in a musical piece or performance.

Tonal center: The pitch in a pitch set given most importance in a melody or scale; primary pitch; tonic.

Tone: A musical sound with a specific pitch, overtone structure, and duration.

Tune: A series of pitches in succession that provide the center of attention in a song or instrumental piece; melody.

Verse: A line or group of lines making up a unit of a sung poem, occasionally preceding a refrain.

Yodel: In singing, rapid alternation between a chest-resonated and head-resonated tone.

References

Blum, Steven. 2000. "Local Knowledge of Musical Genres and Roles." In Timothy Rice et al., eds., *The Garland Encyclopedia of World Music*, vol. 8, Europe, 112–26. New York: Garland.

Buchanan, Donna. 1991. "The Bulgarian Folk Orchestra: Cultural Performance, Symbol, and the Construction of National Identity in Socialist Bulgaria." Ph.D. diss., University of Texas at Austin.

———. 1995. "Metaphors of Power, Metaphors of Truth: The Politics of Music Professionalism in Bulgarian Folk Orchestras." *Ethnomusicology* 39(3):381–416.

———. 1996. "Dispelling the Mystery: The Commodification of Women and Musical Tradition in the Marketing of *Le mystère des voix bulgares*." In Denis P. Hupchick and Donald L. Dryer, eds., *Bulgaria Past and Present: Transitions and Turning Points*. Special issue. *Balkanistica* 9(2):193–210.

———. 1996. "Wedding Musicians, Political Transition, and National Consciousness in Bulgaria." In Mark Slobin, ed., *Retuning Culture: Musical Changes in Central and Eastern Europe*, 200–30. Durham, N.C.: Duke University Press.

———. 1997. Review Essay: "Bulgaria's Magical Mystère Tour: Postmodernism, World Music Marketing, and Political Change in Eastern Europe." *Ethnomusicology* 41(1):131–57.

———. 1999. "Democracy or 'Crazyocracy'? Pirin Folk Music and Sociocultural Change in Bulgaria." In Bruno Reuer, ed., *New Countries, Old Sounds? Cultural Identity and Social Change in Southeastern Europe*, 164–77. Munich: Verlag Südostdeutsches Kulturwerk.

———. 2001. "Bulgaria: Traditional Music." In Stanley Sadie, ed., *The New Grove Dictionary of Music and Musicians*, 2d ed., 4:570–83. London: Grove.

Crampton, R. J. 1997. *A Concise History of Bulgaria*. New York: Cambridge University Press.

Geertz, Clifford. 1973. *The Interpretation of Cultures*. New York: Basic Books.

Krustev, Venelin. 1978. *Bulgarian Music*. Sofia: Sofia Press.

Lausevic, Mirjana. 1998. "A Different Village: International Folk Dance and Balkan Music and Dance in the United States." Ph.D. dissertation, Wesleyan University.

Liegeois, Jean-Paul. 1986. *Gypsies: An Illustrated History.* London: Al Saqi.

Levi, Kler. 2000. "Produtsirane na poslaniia v sŭvremennata 'etnicheska' muzika" [The producing of messages in contemporary "ethnic" music]. *Bulgarian Musicology* 24(3):69–89.

Levy, Mark. 1985. "The Bagpipe in the Rhodope Mountains of Bulgaria." Ph.D. diss., University of California, Los Angeles.

Messner, Gerald Florian. 1980. *Die Schwebungsdiaphonie in Bistrica: Untersuchungen der mehrstimmingen Liedformen eines mittelwestbulgarischen Dorfes.* Tutzing: Schneider.

Poulton, Hugh. 1990. *The Balkans: Minorities and States in Conflict.* London: Minority Rights Publications.

Rice, Timothy. 1977. "Polyphony in Bulgarian Folk Music." Ph.D. diss., University of Washington.

———. 1980. "Aspects of Bulgarian Musical Thought." *Yearbook of the International Folk Music Council* 12:43–67.

———. 1988. "Understanding Three-part Singing in Bulgaria: The Interplay of Concept and Experience." *Selected Reports in Ethnomusicology* 7:43–57.

———. 1994. *May It Fill Your Soul: Experiencing Bulgarian Music.* Chicago: University of Chicago Press.

———. 1996. "The Dialectic of Economics and Aesthetics in Bulgarian Music." In Mark Slobin, ed., *Retuning Culture: Musical Changes in Central and Eastern Europe,* 176–99. Durham, N.C.: Duke University Press.

———. 1997. "Toward a Mediation of Field Methods and Field Experience in Ethnomusicology." In Gregory F. Barz and Timothy J. Cooley, eds., *Shadows in the Field: New Perspectives for Fieldwork in Ethnomusicology,* 101-20. New York: Oxford University Press.

———. 2000. "Béla Bartók and Bulgarian Rhythm." In Elliott Antokoletz et al., eds., *Bartók Perspectives: Man, Composer, and Ethnomusicologist,* 196–210. New York: Oxford University Press.

———. 2000. "Bulgaria." In Timothy Rice et al., eds., *The Garland Encyclopedia of World Music,* vol. 8, *Europe,* 890–910. New York: Garland.

———. 2001. "Reflections on Music and Meaning: Metaphor, Signification, and Control in the Bulgarian Case." *British Journal of Ethnomusicology* 10(1):19–38.

———. 2002. "Bulgaria or Chalgaria: The Attenuation of Bulgarian Nationalism in a Mass-Mediated Popular Music." *Yearbook for Traditional Music* 34:25–46.

————. 2003. "Time, Place, and Metaphor in Musical Ethnography and Experience." *Ethnomusicology* 47(2):151–79.

Silverman, Carol. 1982. "Bulgarian Lore and American Folkloristics: The Case of Contemporary Bulgarian Folk Music." In Walter W. Kolar, ed., *Culture and History of the Bulgarian People: Their Bulgarian and American Parallels*, 65–78. Pittsburgh: Tamburitza Press.

————. 1983. "The Politics of Folklore in Bulgaria." *Anthropological Quarterly* 56(2):55–61.

————. 1986. "Bulgarian Gypsies: Adaptation in a Socialist Context." *Nomadic Peoples* 21/22:51–62.

————. 1989. "Reconstructing Folklore: Media and Cultural Policy in Eastern Europe." *Communication* 11:141–60.

————. 1996. "Music and Marginality: Roma (Gypsies) of Bulgaria and Macedonia." In Mark Slobin, ed., *Retuning Culture: Musical Changes in Central and Eastern Europe*, 231–53. Durham, N.C.: Duke University Press.

————. 2000. "Rom (Gypsy) Music." In Timothy Rice et al., eds., *Garland Encyclopedia of World Music*, vol. 8, *Europe*, 270–93. New York: Garland.

Stoyanova, Maria. 1995. *Gaida Samouchitel: Bagpipe Self-Instructor*. Plovdiv: Akademiya za Muzikalno i Tantsovo Izkustvo.

Taylor, Timothy D. 1997. *Global Pop: World Music, World Markets*. New York: Routledge.

Williams, Raymond. 1977. *Marxism and Literature*. Oxford: Oxford University Press.

Resources

The first place to turn is to the lists of recommended recordings and references on the following pages.

The recordings by Martha Forsyth, A. L. Lloyd, Yves Moreau, and Ethel Raim and Martin Koenig document mainly village music at the local level. The ones by Marcel Cellier contain modern compositions sung by professional choirs, and those by Joe Boyd feature the famous wedding musician Ivo Papazov. Listening to Loren Brody's CD of recordings from the 1920s to the 1940s and comparing those to more recent ones is a great way to understand the effects of modernization on the Bulgarian musical tradition. Many other recordings of professional musicians and ensembles are now available, although as of this writing *popfolk* is notably absent from the market.

Consulting the encyclopedia articles by Buchanan (2001) and Rice (2000) is a good way to broaden the overview presented here and to find more extensive bibliographies. My book, *May It Fill Your Soul: Experiencing Bulgarian Music* (1994), describes in depth the local musical tradition of one family from the Strandzha region and how it was modernized and challenged at the national level during the communist period. A good place to continue the study of the politics of Bulgarian music is Donna Buchanan's 1995 article in the journal *Ethnomusicology*, as well as those by her, Carol Silverman, and me in the book, *Retuning Culture: Music Changes in Central and Eastern Europe* (1996). For more on Bulgarian history, see Crampton (1997). To extend your knowledge of European folk traditions beyond Bulgaria, see *The Garland Encyclopedia of World Music*, vol. 8, *Europe* (2000), which is organized by ethnic groups, nations, and regions and contains useful overview articles as well.

As for films and videos documenting Bulgarian music and dance, three short excerpts, which need to be taken with a grain of salt, have been included on *The JVC Video Anthology of World Music and Dance: Europe III: Romania/Yugoslavia/Bulgaria/Albania*, produced in 1988 by Katsumori Ichikawa for the JVC Victor Company in Tokyo and distributed by Rounder

Records in Cambridge, MA. If you want to learn more about Bulgarian dances, Yves Moreau, one of the leading North American teachers of Bulgarian dance, has produced a series of four videos, available on the internet at www.bourque-moreau.com. Another useful website, www.balkanfolk.net, sells a number of videotapes produced in Bulgaria of professional music and dance ensembles, including the wedding band Kanarite. An 80-minute video, *Le mystère des voix bulgares: A Bird is Singing*, produced in Berlin by Studio K7, documents a 1993 tour of the choral group.

Recommended Recordings

Boyd, Joe. 1991. *Ivo Papazov and His Orchestra: Balkanology.* Hannibal HNCD 1363.

Boyd, Joe, and Rumyana Tzintzarska. 1987. *Balkana: The Music of Bulgaria.* Hannibal HNCD 1335.

———. 1989. *Ivo Papazov and His Bulgarian Wedding Band: Orpheus Ascending.* Hannibal HNCD 1346.

Brody, Lauren. 1998. *Song of the Crooked Dance: Early Bulgarian Traditional Music, 1927–42.* Yazoo Records 7016.

Cellier, Marcel. 1987, 1988. *Le mystère des voix bulgares.* 2 vols. Nonesuch 79165, 79201.

———. 1990. *Le mystère des voix bulgares,* vol. 3. Polygram/Fortuna 846 626.

Forsyth, Martha. 1990. *Two Girls Started to Sing: Bulgarian Village Singing.* Rounder 1055.

Lloyd, A. L. 1959. *Bulgaria.* Columbia KL 5378.

———. 1964. *Folk Music of Bulgaria.* Topic 12T 107.

Moreau, Yves. 1999, 2000, 2001. *Beyond the Mystery: Village Music of Bulgaria.* 3 vols. BMA Productions BMA 1001, 1002, 1003. C.P. 158, Saint-Lambert, Quebec, Canada J4P 3N8.

Music of Bulgaria. 1965. Nonesuch 72011.

Raim, Ethel, and Martin Koenig. 1970a. *A Harvest, a Shepherd, a Bride: Village Music of Bulgaria.* Nonesuch 72034.

———. 1970b. *In the Shadow of the Mountain: Songs and Dances of Pirin-Macedonia.* Nonesuch 72838.

Index

∽